HURRY

GEORDIE STEWART

UP AND WAIT

THE SECRET LIFE OF A SANDHURST CADET

UNICORN

Published in 2022 by Unicorn
an imprint of Unicorn Publishing Group LLP
Charleston Studio
Meadow Business Centre
Lewes BN8 5RW
www.unicornpublishing.org

Text © Geordie Stewart
Illustrator: Olive Sims

ISBN 978-1-914414-96-1

10 9 8 7 6 5 4 3 2 1

Designed by Mach 3 Solutions Ltd (www.mach3solutions.co.uk)
Printed in the UK by Short Run Press, Exeter

HURRY
UP
AND
WAIT

"Sandhurst has adapted and changed since I attended but the fundamentals remain consistent. The camaraderie within your platoon, the special rapport with your instructors and the robustness required to get through it. 'Hurry Up and Wait' is the most accurate and amusing account of Sandhurst I've read."

Sir Chris Bonington

"Funny but true – an observant and human reflection of Sandhurst's benchmark for leadership."

Josh Lewsey MBE

"Irreverent, honest, hilarious, but serious too. Geordie Stewart brilliantly captures the life of a Sandhurst officer cadet. When reluctantly you finish reading this book, you'll know why Sandhurst is so good at its core business of turning out capable leaders, often against the odds. Something it's been doing for over two centuries. Why integrity and respect for others is as important as the more obvious professional skills of the young officer. Stewart describes the individual and collective pleasure of the cadets as they realise that all their hard work is paying off and that they might just be up to commanding people on demanding operations. And of course he describes the intense pride of their families on passing out day.

Military man or simply keen observer of mankind, I cannot recommend this highly readable and authentic book enough."

General Lord Richards of Herstmonceux GCB CBE DSO

"I enjoyed 'Hurry Up and Wait'. Geordie captures the essence of what goes on at Sandhurst, through the eyes of its greatest asset – the young men and women who tread its flagstoned corridors. Humour, heartache, frustration, pride, challenge and adventure; all the ingredients for a cracking read."

Major General Paul Nanson – Sandhurst Commandant 2015-2020 and author of 'Stand Up Straight.'

"Geordie tells the story of Sandhurst just as it is. The Commissioning Course is tough; but then there is nothing easy about being a junior leader in the British Army. The Royal Military Academy maintains the highest of standards; the Academy is among the very best leadership development institutions in the world. And, perhaps without meaning to, this book amplifies that point. It draws out

the madness, the emotion, the challenge, the reward and the humour. It is a triumph. And just as I recall it, as an Officer Cadet and as the Commandant."
Major General David Rutherford-Jones – Sandhurst Commandant
2007-2009

"Sandhurst exerts a fascination. With detail and humour, and an insider's knowledge, Geordie Stewart takes the reader within the machine where the British Army makes its officers."
Simon Akam – Author of 'The Changing of the Guard'

"'Hurry Up and Wait' is a laugh out loud autobiographical comedy. This witty, superbly written book is also a tribute to a grand, sometimes ridiculous, sometimes inspiring institution; by the way – unintentionally perhaps – it's a fine leadership manual.

If you'd like to be an officer in the army, want to know how they are made or are just interested in their often strange world, this book really is, and I appreciate this is an overused phrase, essential reading. 'Hurry Up and Wait' will be, for many years, the classic book on this remarkable British institution."
Frank Ledwidge – Author of 'Losing Small Wars'

"As I read this book, I could imagine my Colour Sergeant standing behind me, ready to make an acerbic remark about the length of my hair.

They say that the only people who enjoy Sandhurst are masochists or liars. But once the pain is forgotten, it is the Senior NCOs that one remembers, determined to turn us 'Civvies' into Officers that they might respect. Any former Officer Cadet, from any era, will recognise themselves in this book and smile, remembering being lambasted for being 'idle' on parade or for being as much use as a 'chocolate frog on a radiator'. I loved this book and promise anyone who has passed out of 'The Idiot Factory', that they will too."
Bryn Parry OBE – Soldier, cartoonist and founder of Help for Heroes

"Geordie writes a very real account about the journey to become a commissioned officer in the British Army. 'Hurry Up and Wait' is a funny, illuminating and authentic story of what life at Sandhurst entails. It made me reflect and laugh as I thought of my own time at the Academy, the framework it provides our future leaders and the lessons I have taken with me since. I highly recommend it to those that want to understand what makes Sandhurst the successful institution it is."
Johnny Mercer MP – Cabinet Minister for Veterans' Affair

"'Hurry Up and Wait' is a distinctive insight into the commissioning course, which brought back my own (mostly happy) memories of Sandhurst. Geordie's account captures the exceptionally funny and intensely serious elements of choosing to serve and lead in the British Army."
Dan Jarvis MBE MP

To all the soldiers I had the privilege to work with, serve under and lead.

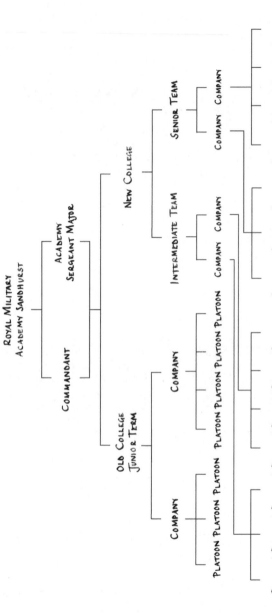

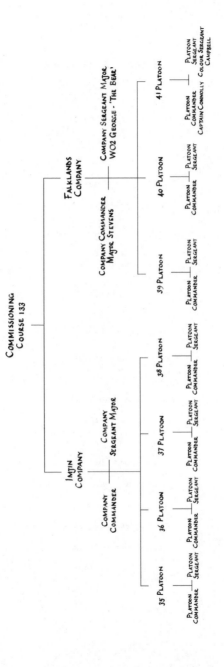

COMMISSIONING COURSE 133

IMJIN COMPANY

COMPANY COMMANDER

COMPANY SERGEANT MAJOR

35 PLATOON
PLATOON COMMANDER
PLATOON SERGEANT

36 PLATOON
PLATOON COMMANDER
PLATOON SERGEANT

37 PLATOON
PLATOON COMMANDER
PLATOON SERGEANT

38 PLATOON
PLATOON COMMANDER
PLATOON SERGEANT

FALKLANDS COMPANY

COMPANY COMMANDER MAJOR STEVENS

COMPANY SERGEANT MAJOR WO2 GEORGE - 'THE BEAR'

39 PLATOON
PLATOON COMMANDER
PLATOON SERGEANT

40 PLATOON
PLATOON COMMANDER
PLATOON SERGEANT

41 PLATOON
PLATOON COMMANDER CAPTAIN CONNOLLY
PLATOON SERGEANT COLOUR SERGEANT CAMPBELL

British Army Ranks

Soldier Ranks

Recruit (Rct)

Private (Pte)

Lance Corporal (L Cpl)

Corporal (Cpl)

Sergeant (Sgt)

Colour Sergeant /
Staff Sergeant (CSgt/SSgt)

Warrant Officer
Class 2 (WO2)

Warrant Officer
Class 1 (WO1)

Officer Ranks

Officer Cadet (O Cdt)

Second Lieutenant (2Lt)

Lieutenant (Lt)

Captain (Capt)

Major (Maj)

Lieutenant Colonel (Lt Col)

Colonel (Col)

Brigadier (Brig)

Major General (Maj Gen)

Lieutenant General (Lt Gen)

General (Gen)

Field Marshal (FM)

Preface

A joy and difficulty in writing about Sandhurst was trying to contextualise an idiosyncratic world and make absurd events relatable. I wrote this book in good spirits and hope all those indirectly referred to receive it as such. With that in mind, all names have been changed to protect the privacy of individuals. To cover my back even further, and to protect me from legal fees that I'd struggle to pay, this is also a story particular to its time and place. Contrary to popular belief, Sandhurst does change, and has in the decade since we inelegantly stumbled around those famous grounds. I have little doubt, however, that the Sandhurst of today retains the same identity, values, ludicrousness and illogicality that baffled, frustrated, motivated and amused me during my time there.

Given the comical number of Army-related terms and acronyms, there is a glossary and an explanation of some of the essential ones at the back of the book – I hope these will help you make sense of things that confused many of us for concerningly long periods. All I can suggest is that you do your best to follow along.

Now that I'm legally and socially armoured up, I hope you enjoy our haphazard journey through Commissioning Course 133 at the Royal Military Academy Sandhurst.

Chapter 1

'ON THE LINE!'

'For fuck's sake!' It's day three of my first week. The words come from the duty cadet worried about fulfilling his own task of rounding everyone up on time. The deep glow of my bedside lamp is partially illuminating my sanitised Sandhurst bedroom. I'm grateful I'm not sharing a room. I fill my Army-issue water bottle to the brim, open the door and see two people rush past. I push open the swinging wooden double doors to the foyer and then the next set to the main corridor. There are 29 young men in green nylon T-shirts, tracksuits and flip-flops lined up against a black tape on the floor: the line. I'm number 27.

It's 5.59 a.m.

Colour Sergeant Campbell stands outside his office in a tracksuit with a cup of tea. 'Numbers!'

We state our numbers in order from 1 to 30. The process is delayed as a few folk are still half asleep. They're met with sideways glances and a chorus of groans as the process begins again. Others, like children in a classroom that want attention, shout louder than anybody else.

'Right, gents, take it away.'

'God save our gracious Queen,
Long live our noble Queen,
God save the Queen!

Send her victorious,
Happy and glorious,
Long to reign over us,
God save the Queen!'

'Water!'

Colour Sergeant Campbell walks along and checks we've got our bottles filled to the brim. For the third day in a row, nobody has let the side down.

'Drink!'

We drink.

'Why do we do that?' Nobody answers. 'I can't keep asking myself questions, gents.'

Someone near the middle answers, 'So we remain hydrated and show our loyalty to the Queen, Colour Sergeant?'

'Aye, Mr...' The 'mister' is drawn out as Colour Sergeant Campbell moves along the line and looks directly at the person who's spoken.

'Hammond, Colour Sergeant.'

'Aye, Mr Hammond, so we show our loyalty to the Queen... your new boss. Anyone else?'

'So we're up early together.'

'Thank you, Mr... '

'Norton.'

'Early? I thought you'd thank me for the extra sleep, Mr Norton.'

'Thank you, sir.'

'My pleasure, Mr Norton. And it shall continue to be my pleasure throughout Commissioning Course 133 here at the Royal Military Academy Sandhurst.' He continues while patrolling in front of us. 'Gents, it's better to check than trust. Hydration is key. No water and you'll go man down. Go man down and you could become *deed*. Or worse, combat ineffective.' The emphasis is very much on the 'in' in ineffective but, given the Glaswegian lilt, it comes across more as *aneffective*.

'Next timing: breakfast at 0700 hours. A final thing. Mr Norton, don't call me sir. I actually work for a living. Training programme is on the board. You're in your own time now, gents.'

It's been non-stop since I arrived on Sunday: a crammed schedule, and we're always moving. And if we're not moving, we're changing from one outfit to another to then move again. From coveralls to combats to exercise kit; from the parade square to the swimming pool to the dining hall. The only time we stop is to sleep, and even then, we're worried about crumpling our pristinely ironed sheets; some have even slept on the floor. This is the infamous first five weeks, and even though we partially knew what to expect, we're all like rabbits in the headlights.

This is the start of Commissioning Course (CC) 133 at the Royal Military Academy Sandhurst (RMAS), the finest and most well-respected military training establishment in the world. This 44-week leadership course is designed to mould the future officers of the British Army. Its status as 'the national centre of excellence for leadership' is a bold claim but it's very Sandhurst. The Academy is unlikely to settle for second best.

Three times per year – January, May and September – this 44-week social experiment takes place: take around two hundred fit, willing and able volunteers, subject them to a rigorous training schedule and analyse the results. Attendees know it as the 'Factory', 'Sandbags', or 'Camberley Technical College'. Annually around six hundred young men and women are given a commission signed by the head of state and become British Army officers.

Until the creation of the New Model Army by Oliver Cromwell in 1645, England never actually had a professional standing army. Instead, it relied on private forces, mercenaries or militias organised by local officials. For foreign expeditions, troops were raised on an ad hoc basis when required by the ruling monarch but there were minimal full-time soldiers.

A few hefty defeats in the Napoleonic Wars precipitated a mentality shift in military training. Until that point, most leadership positions were assigned based on social status and titles, but it transpired that not all British aristocrats exhibited the required military competence to fulfill their roles. As such, greater emphasis was placed on leadership and ability as the military was forced to professionalise. Since 1947, Sandhurst has been where all British Army Officers have conducted their training.

The list of achievements of former Sandhurst attendees is impressive. There have been astronauts, Olympians, explorers, authors, poets and musicians. A wide array of domestic and foreign politicians can also count Sandhurst as part of their education. Prior to joining, you're told by others it must be some-thing in the Sandhurst water that helps mould such an array of talented alumni. It isn't. Sandhurst is located 30 miles from Central London in Hampshire just off the M3 motorway and is surrounded by Fleet, Farnborough, Woking and Bracknell. The water clearly isn't the differentiating factor.

There are pros and cons to each of the three commissioning course intakes and it's principally determined by the British climate. January starts and ends unpleasantly, making the tran-sition from civilian life quite an affronting winter experience. May is congenial and this course is seen, perhaps incorrectly, as being more relaxed. Out of sheer practicality, I've started in September. Unfortunately, this is picked by many 'thrusty' types who enact their long-term military career plan at the earliest opportunity. Many of the September intake have done University

Officers' Training Corps (UOTC) – Army Reserve for university students and pronounced 'core' as opposed to 'corpse' – or have served as officers in the Reserve. This group get it, whatever *it* is. They're thoroughbreds – keen, knowledgeable folk who think as you're meant to think and indeed likely want to think that way. Sandhurst needs these people. I'm not one of them.

I'm what's known as a 'military virgin'. No Reserve, no cadets, no military experience at all. I have known a lot of Army folk and have diligently prepared for selection, but I know little about such things as the dimensions of the latest Russian tank or the muzzle velocity of the new Israeli machine gun. For me, this is entering a new world, with a new language where even the acronyms have acronyms: TLA stands for 'three-letter acronym'. I have minimal understanding of the terminology, the routines or the lifestyle. I don't *need* to know these things – I have only started a few days before. But some people do know those things. They know the lingo, how to march, handle a rifle, pack a bergen (what the fuck is a bergen?) and mould a beret. And that means we military virgins have plenty to learn.

We are informed that Sandhurst has a 'learn by doing' philosophy. What quickly becomes apparent is that a steep learning/ doing curve awaits. Thankfully, I'm not the only one in this position. Many have started this journey before and made it through. For now, though, the conductor's whistle has blown, the doors have shut, the train is moving. It will make it to the next station. I have to ensure that this floundering passenger will somehow still be on board.

In a utopian world, we wouldn't need armies. There'd be no guns, bombs, coups or wars – peace and serenity would prevail. Human history, however, tells a different story: power struggles, aggressors, expansionists. There has been democracy, communism, socialism, oligarchy, autocracy, monarchy, theocracy, colonialism; and then there's Christianity, Islam, Hinduism, Buddhism, Sikhism, Judaism, Taoism, Shinto and so on. In short, it transpires that not all humans think the same, which inevitably leads to conflict.

At the turn of the 20th century, the British Army had around five hundred thousand full-time personnel. This number spiked up to five million during the two World Wars but has been gradually declining since: four hundred thousand in 1967, three hundred thousand in 1990 and two hundred thousand in 2005. Nowadays, the British Army comprises around seventy thousand full-time and more than thirty thousand Reserve personnel. Its commander-in-chief is Queen Elizabeth II. According to the MOD website, its purpose is to protect the UK, prevent conflict, deal with disaster and fight the nation's enemies. The official line continues, 'From preventing terrorism to providing humanitarian aid to people in need, the British Army is driven to make the world a safer, better place.' As remits go, it's a broad one.

⌐ — ⌐

Growing up near Army Headquarters in Andover and close to Salisbury Plain, seeing Army vehicles and uniformed folk around was not uncommon. My grandfathers and great grandfathers were in the military; I remember the black-and-white photos of them at home. There was something both intimidating and distinguished about their look: pressed uniforms, aligned medals, smart haircuts, stern expressions. As a child with little regard for rules, that's how I viewed them. For a teenager with a similar disposition, the Army had little appeal as a long-term aspiration; it was too formal, too constraining. I still looked, admittedly with intrigue, from the outside but without a yearning to pursue it. And then a few friends and friends of friends joined. They were invariably sent on operations to Iraq or Afghanistan. Front pages at the time were covered with images of coffins draped in the Union Flag and homecoming parades, while fundraising ventures for wounded veterans were common; all occurred alongside unprecedented stories of selflessness, bravery, pride and teamwork. To an adventurous young man, the Army began to appear more honourable and worthy.

My attitude fundamentally altered on a mountaineering expedition during university. Climbing with, and living alongside, a few current and former soldiers for several months gave me a new insight. I had officers and soldiers, Royal Marines and Lynx helicopter pilots next to me. They exhibited an unspoken understanding, humour and mindset that differentiated them from others – a willingness to get stuck in and endure, combined with teamwork and conscientiousness. If the Army formed that, I thought, sign me up.

I decided to try to become an officer. Leadership, decision-making and taking responsibility seemed the right path for me. And this is where Sandhurst fits in. In theory, Sandhurst is where you learn to lead and manage soldiers. You also learn technical military skills including everything from how to fire and keep your rifle serviceable to how to command an infantry attack irrespective of which branch of the Army you choose to commit to.

Getting into Sandhurst is not a given. First, I needed to pass Army Officer Selection Board (AOSB), a process designed to select candidates with the potential to become Army officers.

Before that, and before online applications became a reality, I had to fill out innumerable forms explaining my rationale for joining, education, qualifications, role preferences, interests and anything else mildly appropriate. Half a tree of paperwork later, I had rubbed out the pencilled lines in each box, avoided any blotting from the black ink I was required to use and painstakingly scrutinised my own application. I then needed the green light from my Army careers advisor, an interview I erroneously planned during freshers' week in my penultimate year at university.

My phone alarm goes off. My brain can barely process the inconsiderate and unavoidable noise let alone locate the source to shut the thing up. A period of apologetic, blurry-eyed and expletive-filled fumbling ensues. The 8 a.m. time and 7 per cent battery provoke a startling change of momentum. With less than 60 minutes until handshakes, my body and mind spark into life. I throw on my clothes from the night before, run home, shower, change into a pair of chinos and a partially ironed shirt, grab my car keys and get the wheels rolling.

At 8.55 a.m., a besuited, middle-aged man walks towards me with an arm outstretched. 'Geordie, I presume. Good morning. Come on in.'

If I don't smell of booze, then the stale cigarettes must be obvious. I can't find a bin. I swallow my chewing gum. I'm reminded of my mum saying it'll never digest.

I'm expecting a cup of tea and a bit of signposting about the next steps. Instead, I gratefully accept a mug of instant black coffee and for three hours I'm signing forms, discussing the president of the International Monetary Fund, evaluating potential military intervention in Syria, dissecting my character traits, suitability for different regiments and leadership potential. Have I got away with it? I reckon I might have.

As we part, the retired lieutenant colonel – pronounced 'leftenant' as opposed to 'loo-tenant' – sticks out a hand, gives a firm handshake, looks me intently in the eye and says, 'Geordie, good to meet you. We'll be in touch.'

Do I call him colonel, Mr Longstaff or sir? 'Thank you, I look forward to it.' Circumvention seems a safe strategy.

'And, Geordie, one quick bit of advice. Look at how I'm dressed and look at how you're dressed. Best we leave it at that, wouldn't you agree? Have a good rest of freshers' week and do ensure you're safe to drive before you arrange any further interviews. Speak soon.'

And just like that, the door shuts and I'm put firmly back in my box.

To my surprise and relief, the lieutenant colonel (retd) emailed that afternoon saying he had enjoyed meeting me. Our electronic back and forth continued over the following days and weeks. Having tried a few different openings – Dear Lt Col Longstaff, Dear Colonel Longstaff, Dear Col Longstaff, Colonel, and even Hi Colonel (bold!) – I was informed that 'Dear Colonel' was the correct option. Confusingly, he began with 'Geordie' every time.

Relieved to be given the green light, I proceeded to the next step and was now ready to attend AOSB at Westbury in Wiltshire.

Chinos, shirt, tie, tweed jacket. The attire was 'recommended' rather than required. In the spirit of, 'If you can't beat 'em, join 'em', I found myself thus attired alongside 50 or so other potential officers. This was Part One of AOSB, known as Briefing: 24 hours of assessments, interviews, physicals, practical tests and presentations.

The 50 of us were sitting in what looked like a 3-star British country pub lounge area adorned with aged leather armchairs and sofas in convenient circles of around six to eight people but without the sodden dogs and roaring fire. Military paintings in dark brown frames lined the walls. A sergeant – Welsh chap from Llanberis with 15 years of service – lightened the mood, made a few quips and gave a few briefs. Welcome to the world of Army banter. Each of us was assigned a group and corresponding bib colour. With our tribal identification secured, we had individual mugshots and a team photo taken. We spent an hour outside in tracksuits completing a team 'command task', where we had to get all members and a 'burden' – a randomly chosen item for command tasks only, often a stretcher or a 20-kilogram ammunition box – from point A to point B without touching the ground, using only a couple of planks of wood, a small oil drum and some rope. We had interviews, lectures and medicals, completed psychometric tests and were told to be ourselves to assess our compatibility with military life. We delivered a presentation and took part in a suitably awkward current affairs discussion.

At the end, we each fell into one of four categories. Category 1: You are ready to attend Main Board (Part Two of AOSB). You can continue to play Army snakes and ladders. Have another roll of the dice. Category 2: You require a delay before progressing to address specific areas of your performance. Category 3: You 'could' pass but require 'considerable improvement'. Category 4: You are unlikely to be successful at Main Board and are therefore unsuitable for officer selection. You've landed on a snake and are sliding down. No more throws of the dice.

Not feeling confident as to how I'd fared, I was thankful to make the cut for Category 1. In preparation for Main Board, I completed more paperwork in black ink answering the same previously answered questions. University life continued simultaneously – alcohol and parties, precisely the wrong way to prepare, when I should have been practicing and training. But I regularly ran, cycled, did press-ups, sit-ups and bleep tests – the latter a procedure used to estimate your aerobic capacity that involves running progressively quicker back and forth over a 20-metre distance.

To prepare for the mental arithmetic aspect of selection, I delved into my academic memory bank to begin the process of remembering how to find 'X' in an algebraic equation. Then there was long multiplication and division. Does that number carry over or remain where it is? What about decimal places? I obsessed about time-distance-speed questions. The sort of 'You and your family travel 100 miles to see your relatives at Christmas. The return journey takes 4 hours 30 minutes. How fast were you driving?' We knew these questions would be asked – we just had to remember how to be a 15-year-old revising for their Maths exams.

I wrote current affairs essays, recorded presentations and began a PLANEX.* This is a military planning exercise in which you're given a large chunk of text – usually a story about an incident in a remote location. You must analyse the details: deadlines, land masses, distances, personnel, threats, terrain types, equipment, requirements and objectives, before making a plan to save the day.

I was nervy driving down to Westbury for the four-day Main Board assessment. Succeed and that's it: you get a place at Sandhurst. I didn't want to think about failing but it was hard not to. I felt prepared but worried. Was I fit and smart enough? Were the many hours of preparation enough?

A few familiar faces were present from Briefing and we made self-conscious small talk. The same short Welsh sergeant attempted to ease the tension with his jokes about cavalry officers playing polo, Guards officers wearing red trousers and the Parachute Regiment having a chip on their shoulder. Soon after, we were allocated bibs and numbers. Red 53. First requirement: a bleep test. A few failed. After changing back into our suits, they were packing their bags. We *had* been warned.

The sergeant marched us into a lecture theatre. It was unmistakably group walking but those in the know attempted to remain 'in step' with their arms extending beyond what's usually expected of a walker while the rest of us ambled uncomfortably

---

*   Please excuse the random capitalisations – it's Army doctrine.

close to the people around us. We sat down and chatted idly, until he shouted, 'BRACE UP!' A few people sat bolt upright and extended their arms rigidly with their clenched fists placed on their knees. The rest of us awkwardly followed suit.

The colonel, who must have been attentively lurking within earshot just outside the room, decided to enter. He was middle-aged, wore glasses and had thinning grey hair, twenty years or so of service under his belt and a bit of a paunch. He and the Welshman saluted each other a few times and stamped their feet a bit before the colonel told us to sit 'At ease'. We dutifully unclenched our fists and resumed our previous pose. A pleasantly succinct brief followed along the lines of 'This is where it all begins', 'I remember being in your shoes' and 'Give it your best shot.' We played the 'Brace up!' and 'At ease' game again as he and the Welshman engaged in a second round of arm-waving and foot-stamping.

We were marched into a larger room akin to a school examination hall. We wrote a current affairs essay – mine happened to be on the Scottish nationalism debate – before conducting several hours of psychometric tests – numeracy, literacy and abstract – similar to those at Briefing but more complex and in more depth. With a canteen dinner and shared dorm later, day one was complete.

Day two began with wake up at 6 a.m., or 0600 hours – zero six hundred – that is. For a student, incomprehensibly early. In reality, it was pre-0600 as one keen bean in our room decided to get ahead in the shower/shaving queue. This led to a) a decline in his popularity and b) us getting even less sleep than the little we had planned for. Regardless, up we got and changed into suits for the day ahead.

More current affairs followed, this time in a group format as we discussed Obama, drones and taxes as well as the

Nuclear Non-Proliferation Treaty, the EU and NATO, sitting in a circle on plastic chairs while fluorescent strip lights flickered on the ceiling above. The lack of knowledge and confidence in some was starkly contrasted by the precise language and assuredness of others. Having some involvement was necessary. We all knew that. And if that meant rewording and reiterating a previous point then those tactics were willingly adopted by many. Cagey vanilla opinions were prudently and tentatively voiced while internal sentiments were wisely kept subsurface.

Onto the next test and in a scene more akin to a dentist's waiting area, I cooled my heels with a few others as people came in and out of different rooms. Usually there was a sigh, shrug or smile as they transitioned through. Three interviews followed: two with mid- and senior-ranking officers and a third, the one we dreaded most, with the Education Officer. We hardly helped ourselves by recounting rumours about him speaking to you in German, French, Italian and Spanish if you'd put a foreign language on your CV, or cross-examining your cultural knowledge if you'd expressed an interest in the arts. A thorough examination of our capacity for quick thinking, intellectual ability and cultural knowledge was anticipated.

'Mr Stewart, please come in.'

I took a breath, looked him in the eye and shook hands. I waited for him to sit behind his solid wooden desk before taking my place opposite. He shuffled around a few papers and I watched his eyes scan the information before him.

'Hmmm, I've seen better school exam results.'

'Yes, sir, you probably have. I wouldn't say I fully applied myself.'

'Indeed, that much is obvious. Clearly not a fan of languages then, either?'

'In all honesty, I probably find greater comfort in my own language.'

'Clearly.' The Education Officer peered at me above his half-moon spectacles. It was the sort of inquisitive look a headmaster might give you.

'So, Geordie, what book are you currently reading?'

'A biography of the great Brazilian Formula One driver, Ayrton Senna.'

'A great driver indeed. What a tragedy. And who wrote this biography?'

'Good question. I can't remember.'

'Ah, yes. Like all great authors... anonymous.' I received the peer over the glasses. He jotted a few notes down on the papers in front of him.

'And, Geordie, what's your favourite film?'

'*Shawshank Redemption*, I'd say.' I'm not sure why I said that – an excellent film but not my favourite.

Oh no, the same look. Those bloody glasses.

'Hmmm, I've heard that one a few times.' He wrote in a small box on the form.

I realised the interview was not going well. Thus far, I'd come across as unoriginal, ignorant and stupid: an unenviable combination.

'Hold that thought please, sir. My answer was a lie. My favourite films would probably be *Notting Hill*, *The Lion King*, *Cool Runnings*, *Lord of the Rings* and *No Direction Home*.' Rom-com, Disney, comedy, fantasy... and a three-and-a-half-hour documentary about Bob Dylan.

'Hmmm, interesting.' *That* look. But it lasted even longer. I considered walking out and calling a premature end to the misery. It was better to jump than be pushed.

'Very good, Geordie. A far more honest and informative answer. I've always preferred my childhood films. As for Bob Dylan, I prefer his work from the mid-60s to what he produced afterwards but that's a debate for another day. I'll add *No Direction Home* to my list.'

The interview proceeded in a smoother manner as we discussed theatre productions, music, language and degree choices. He then shuffled his papers around a bit, placed one hand on top of the other and looked at me over his glasses once more.

'So, Geordie, you're driving home on a motorway. The journey takes you three hours and thirty minutes. You stick to seventy miles per hour the whole way. How far have you travelled?'

I knew the formula: $D = S \times T$. *Did I put the hours into minutes or not? Was it 70×210? That couldn't be correct. It had to be 70×3.5. That seemed more realistic. $70 \times 3 = 210$. Half of 70 was 35. $210 + 35 = 245$.*

'Two hundred and forty-five miles, sir.' I thought I was right. It seemed *about* right. London to St Andrews was almost five hundred miles and it took around nine hours. I was in the right ballpark. Slowly his head lowered and tilted slightly to the right exaggerating his double chin. It was a painfully slow nod.

'Correct, well done.' I strained to see what he jotted down. 'Unless you have any further questions, that's all from me, Geordie. Thank you.' I stood up, shook his hand and left the room relieved.

That afternoon we hit the command tasks outside. We were dressed in our overalls and red bibs ready for physical activities. As before, these were leaderless tasks – versions of getting the ammo box/burden/casualty from A to B without touching the ground. As with the group discussions, everyone needed to contribute; silence was self-sabotage. And importantly, we weren't allowed to use our names – we were our numbers and our numbers were us. Like the host in the TV show *The Crystal Maze* or a school PE teacher, our instructor moved our group around to eye up one potential task after another. He then read the rules for the task and said how long we had to complete it. He started the stopwatch, opened his notebook and observed proceedings from a few metres away.

For most people, this was a fresh command task challenge and, soon after the instructor's stopwatch began, there was a surreal unspoken race for the role of timekeeper. With just five minutes to find a solution to the task, seconds counted, and the time-keeper's sole purpose in that period was to update the team on their remaining time. Some would throw in percentages along-side inane expressions of encouragement such as 'Good work, guys, we're twenty per cent of the way through' to appear useful. This was smart; they had shown mental arithmetic and leadership potential. While some thought they could sod off, in the game of Army officer selection, the timekeeper won.

With each task about completion, but also the minimisation of mistakes, another potentially decisive role was that of quality control expert. As with the timekeeper, this was not an official role but was treated as such by those who voluntarily took on the responsibility, and thereby appeared to play a critical role in the team's success. This selection thruster gave reminders such as 'Let's keep our discipline here, lads' and other comparable state-ments. The input of Mr 'State the Fucking Obvious' was rightly derided by the team but commended by the instructors.

With so many roles up for grabs, it did beg the question of how any task was actually completed. Thankfully, this was usually solved by a keen former cadet with prior knowledge delivered during a lull in group planning. We then enacted the said plan with gusto while ensuring we moved the burden, helped others and voiced encouragement.

The next day, another unpleasant 6 a.m. alarm was followed by last-minute cramming and being herded into the lecture hall for a PLANEX. The scenario we were allotted involved rescuing a friend, Helen, who was seriously wounded after a car crash. There was a deadline for her to reach medical treatment with several possible means of transport and routes varying in length, terrain and safety. For 75 minutes, silently at our desks, we individually puzzled over various other factors too: the weather forecast, medical supplies, water, fuel, bandits, swamps and support. Time-distance-speed calculations were needed alongside correct prioritisation, balancing risk and adaptability. As when an examiner says, 'Time's up, pens down', there was an audible sigh of relief upon the final tick of the clock. Anxiety swept over most of us as errors were quickly realised during the post-mortem outside the lecture hall. We then moved back to our red-bib classroom for a full analysis before presenting an aligned Course of Action (COA) to the group leader. Mercifully our collective brains allowed Helen to receive the required medical treatment in the seven-hour window she needed to avoid a premature visit to the pearly gates.

After a post-PLANEX recovery lunch, it was time to put aside our thoughts of Helen's welfare and mental arithmetic. We headed back outside in our ill-fitting coveralls and white helmets for more command tasks. For this phase, the challenges were the same but there was an assigned leader rather than a group plan.

A notable highlight occurred when a member of our group, number 52, suggested a plan that involved throwing a rope over a cross beam. The seconds and minutes ticked by as we observed him diligently tying a sizeable knot at one end. Several practice swings later and he was ready. One, two, three... the vicious weight was released from his hand. Instead of soaring mightily, however, it drastically altered course. At the time, the visiting colonel was making polite small talk to a nearby captain. The expression on number 52's face swiftly altered from surprise to horror as the colonel's sternum received the full force of the projectile. In slow motion, he was whipped off his feet, his arms and legs floating upwards before inelegantly joining his fallen body on the ground. He gingerly removed the weapon that lay over him and rose with his brown beret askew, then hobbled away refusing support, angry, embarrassed and in pain. The timekeeper reminded us that our time was up. Number 52 was motionless and speechless.

They are not looking for the finished product at AOSB. The assessors are analysing your *potential* to communicate with, lead, manage and motivate your soldiers. The point of AOSB is to allow people to express their strengths and show what they might be capable of. As the retired lieutenant colonel had said to me, 'Be yourself, but the best of yourself.' These were wise words to bear in mind when approaching any interview.

We had hazy heads the next morning after the formal mess dinner on the final night. Nevertheless, we managed to complete the closing race – an inter-team command task competition – and our mid-table mediocrity was satisfactory before we changed and received a final lecture from the bespectacled colonel. He reminded us of the privilege of leading soldiers, congratulated us for making it to the end of selection and wished us the best for the letters being posted that afternoon. We were then put 'At ease' a final time before being released from camp, free to anxiously await the outcome of our efforts.

I returned home and gave my family an overview of the past few days. I was hopeful, not expectant. When I returned from a damp dog walk after a lazy morning, a letter was sitting on the kitchen table – the crisp cream envelope with neat handwriting on the outside was unmistakably formal. My mum was lurking nearby pretending to be busy. I carefully opened the letter looking for the first word which I expected to be either 'Congratulations' or 'Unfortunately'.

It read:

Dear Geordie,
Congratulations. You have been successful in passing the
Army Officer Selection Board.

The rest of the letter was insignificant; the overall result was all
I cared about. Relief swept over me. Relief I had not failed, had
not let anyone down and now knew what my overall career plan
would look like for the next few years. I experienced a touch of
personal satisfaction as I told my family and passed on the news
to those who had helped me achieve the positive result through
support, advice or sharing personal experiences. I wasn't sure how
other red bibbers had fared but I hoped perhaps our paths might
cross again 30 miles west of London.

In the process of the paperwork going back and forth, the
return trips to Westbury and the many conversations and hours
spent in preparation, I hadn't fully taken stock of what it all
meant. All those questions about problem-solving, risk management, analysis and leadership were gatekeepers to my safe and
suitable passage to the next square in the game of Army: the
Royal Military Academy Sandhurst. The continual tests of intel-
lect, command and planning were methods to test my motivation and potential ability to lead soldiers in the most demanding
situations. It was almost absurd to think about post-Sandhurst
life when I had only just been accepted but impossible not to.
Commissioning and becoming an officer was the aim but far
more immediate challenges lay ahead.

Chapter 2

The start of Sandhurst is known as 'Ironing Board Sunday'. Mum, my girlfriend Sophie and I drove down together. The car was full to the brim with items and accessories I had not thought about or used for years. The day before, I had purchased a set of stencils, an array of permanent markers with different nib colours and sizes, a protractor, compass, rubber, pencil sharpener and 90-degree ruler. Added to that list were lever arch folders, waterproof folders, A4 pads of paper and notebooks. I had even managed to source a never-before-heard-of 'chinograph pencil' costing £1.50 – apparently necessary for taking notes in the rain. Into the pencil case it went. It felt like going back to school, or more aptly, starting at a new school, with an added sense of dread and anxiety.

I also needed two knife, fork and spoon (KFS) sets – one for display, one for use. I had a spare toothbrush, toothpaste and razor for inspection days. I had Brasso, Silvo and every other conceivable polish you could find, plus a swathe of brushes, a sewing kit, dusters, laundry bags and washing capsules. I spent ages googling 'best iron reviews' before plumping for a 4.7-star Morphy Richards 'easy-to-use, steam-generating, crease-eliminating, time-minimising, effortlessly effective' iron. As the gear piled up, my immediate future began to look worryingly like a weighty combination of housework and academia.

I also required non-military clothing. A suit: traditional cut and double-vented; shoes: black Oxford; shirts: double cuff; ties:

nothing garish. I needed chinos ('Avoid red, unless you want to appear a complete knob' was the recommendation), a tweed jacket and brown shoes. I needed at least ten wooden hangers (emphasis was always placed on the material), shorts, Speedos and a set of goggles.

The military-specific kit was different again. Map cases, a metal mug, spare socks, a waterproof notepad, a Nyrex (a waterproof folder), a head torch, a model-making kit, tent pegs, knee pads and a compass.

Then there were the medical supplies: plasters, zinc oxide tape, Compeed, painkillers, scissors, tweezers and antiseptic cream.

There was one more addition to prepare me for a year living behind barbed wire: the ironing board.

I spoke with sales assistants and prepared myself physically by carting around catalogues and testing different iron and ironing board combinations in department stores. In the end I went for a Sandhurst classic: a Brabantia Titan coming in at a nervy £69.99, reduced from £119.99 in the late-summer sales. Its 'heat-resistant iron zone' combined with a 'sturdy asymmetric frame with protective non-slip feet caps' and 'adjustable height options' – from 61 to 102 centimetres – made it hard to go past. It was a necessary item, but such a high-end version? Maybe that *could* make the difference between poor and satisfactory when it came to room inspections. Into the car it went.

We grabbed a coffee on the way to kill time (Mum had insisted we leave early so as not to arrive late). I had visited Sandhurst once before, on the Pre-Commissioning Course Briefing Course, effortlessly abbreviated to the roll-off-the-tongue acronym, PCCBC. That had been a two-day visit to listen to lectures and, for fear of social shaming, inevitably not ask the questions we wanted answering. We'd been provided with our new combat boots and told to break them in to prevent blisters. We had the entertaining experience of another Army medical which entailed the schoolboy-doctor classic: the cough and drop.

We peeled off the A30, went through the open gates and joined the short queue of cars in the 'No Passes' line by the main entrance. I entered the guardhouse, signed a form with our names and car registration and we proceeded up the road with thick over-hanging branches blocking the sun. There was a murky lake to the left. The signs said, '10mph'. We took the left fork in the road labelled CC133. In front of us emerged the iconic wide rectangular building of Old College with a Union Flag flying at full mast above the imposing pillars and famous Old College steps.

The road bent to the right and we parked next to a grey Audi A4 and behind a blue Ford Focus. Young men in suits exited each passenger door. They opened the boots and both cars were also filled to the brim. The three of us removed our ironing boards and shared a moment of mutual acknowledgment. A uniformed young man with a clipboard came over.

'I assume you're starting today, sir?' he asked, to which I nodded, still slightly taken aback by the 'sir'. 'If you could please head that way, sir, you'll be directed by someone at the Old College steps.'

Sophie and I took a photo by one of the canons captured at the Battle of Waterloo. I'm in a navy suit, blue tie, white shirt and black shoes. My haircut is short and smart. She's standing next to me smiling, proud and elegant. A few months before, we had stayed together in a little cottage in Brecon for a week. We went for long walks with the dogs, swam in the river, tended to the plants, played cards and savoured long baths and lazy mornings. A lovely holiday; respite before ridicule. We spoke of the difficulties of those coming first five weeks, the alternate weekends we could see each other, the fortnightly breaks between terms, the post-Sandhurst holiday and life beyond. But neither of us really knew what lay ahead. Even at this stage, that apocryphal

Sandhurst statistic popped into my head: 80 per cent of cadets start with a girlfriend and 20 per cent smoke. By the end, 80 per cent smoke and 20 per cent have a girlfriend. I neglected to share it with her. I believed we would be different.

Mum and Sophie were signposted one way, us the other. I signed a few forms and was given a yellow badge with blue writing saying 'STEWART'. My ironing board and I were directed to our accommodation: the block. My room was unloved and soulless with bare cupboards, thin pale curtains, a single bed in one corner and a sink in the other. I switched my suit and shirt for an ill-fitting green coverall with my yellow name tag over my heart. We were reunited with our guests and I took another picture with Sophie. This time I felt self-conscious, on edge, apprehensive. She laughed at me affectionately. A few other couples were doing the same. I was then ready to be left alone; I needed to get on with it. I gave my mum a hug and said, 'Thank you.' Sophie and I kissed and shared a long hug.

I went back to my room and kept my door propped open for fear of missing any information. A few others lurked in the corridor. Then I heard those three words for the first time: 'On the line!' It meant nothing until someone poked their head around the door and beckoned my neighbour and me into an adjacent corridor where a jumble of young men waited.

A man in uniform told us to stand against the wall. On his rank slide were the three chevrons of a sergeant with a crown on top. He wore a green Tam o'Shanter with a green hackle. A Tam o'Shanter is a traditional Scottish bonnet worn by men. The name derives from Tam o'Shanter, the eponymous hero of the 1790 Robert Burns poem. It's the equivalent of a beret for those in the Scottish regiments.

In a thick Glaswegian accent, the man in uniform said, 'Afternoon, gents', before asking, 'How yous doing today?' It might have been a rhetorical question, it might not. Nobody replied. 'Right chatty bunch yous are. I'm Colour Sergeant Campbell, 5 SCOTS, and I'm colour sergeant of yous lot: 41 Platoon, Falklands Company.'

That was the first I had heard from a Sandhurst colour sergeant, any colour sergeant, in fact, but the Sandhurst ones had a particular reputation: feared and respected in equal measure. They, he, would provide the backbone of our training throughout our commissioning course. 'You never forget your Sandhurst colour sergeant,' we'd been told. Well, this Scotsman opposite us struck me, at first meeting, as a man who might leave his mark.

We were then sent away for 'scoff' – a meal in civvy, or civilian, speak – of spaghetti bolognaise with a few salad leaves guiltily lurking around, before Colour Sergeant Campbell got us to the line. In alphabetical order – Agnew at one end and Yarrow at the other – we took a seat on either side of the corridor, legs outstretched. Agnew was given number 1, Yarrow 30. I was number 27.

We proceeded with an ice breaker – each of us standing to give a brief introduction about who we were, our experiences and an interesting fact. A sort of 'Hi, I'm Jonathan Travers. I'm 23 years old. I did Business Studies at Newcastle University. I was in the OTC at university. Interesting fact… I've swum with sharks off the coast of Australia on my gap year.' Or 'Hi, I'm Josh Reagan and I'm 21 years old. I went to Welbeck College followed by Loughborough University. My dad was a major in the Royal Signals. I'm a second lieutenant in the Army Reserve. I've always wanted to come to Sandhurst full-time and my interesting fact is that I've competed for the Army at orienteering.' Probably like most, I have an aversion to ice breakers so was pleased to sit back down again after a brief opening: 'Hi, I'm Geordie Stewart. I'm 24, graduated from the University of St Andrews and would also go into the military virgin category. Interesting fact: I completed the National Three Peaks Challenge last month.'

Of the seven platoons in CC133, six were all male and one was all female*. Of the three platoons in Falklands Company, including ours, all three were male, and the majority of our platoon were white, middle class and university-educated – around 85 per cent of Sandhurst cadets are graduates. There were four foreign cadets: Mardirossoyan from Armenia, Al-Tabari from Iraq, Shahid from Abu Dhabi and Naj Abil from Afghanistan. Each platoon at Sandhurst has three or four foreign cadets. This tradition has continued for generations and is based on the concepts of international cooperation and foreign partnership-building.

'Gents, get ta bed now. Water parade on the line at 0600. Welcome to the Royal Military Academy Sandhurst. Sleep well.' Then our colour sergeant departed through the wooden doors and out of sight. There were mutterings between us before we each traipsed back to our rooms.

Ironing Board Sunday was when so many of those hopes, fears, expectations, nerves and excitements about a career as an Army officer began. It was the same for everyone who had done that same journey, taken those same pictures and said those same farewells, likely with their own versions of the Brabantia Titan under their arms.

I looked at the three black kitbags still sitting in the middle of my floor. I looked at my watch. I thought about when I would need to be up in the morning for day one, week one. I brushed my teeth, set my alarm for 0550 and got under my sheets to sleep.

<hr />

* All Sandhurst platoons are now fully integrated.

0550. The alarm woke me abruptly – anything pre-0600 was grim. More alarms sounded from adjacent rooms before doors opened. I put on my tracksuit bottoms, an Army-issue T-shirt and flip-flops. Colour Sergeant Campbell had said to never walk around the corridors without flip-flops; something about clean feet and spreading infections. I filled my one-litre water bottle to the brim and twisted the black cap shut. I took my position next to Number 26, Simpson. Number 20, Norton, rushed past at 0559 and into line.

'Right, numbers,' said Colour Sergeant Campbell. We read out 1 to 30 with questionable eagerness. 'Gents, is anyone in this morning? Let's try one more time.' We called our numbers in order again. It didn't require a third attempt.

'National anthem,' he said. We sang 'God Save the Queen'.

'Water bottles.' We each unscrewed our water bottle caps. Colour Sergeant Campbell moved along the line checking the water level. 'Drink,' he said. We drank.

'Satisfactory. Next timing, gents: breakfast at 0700.'

Unlike most military academies, Sandhurst entrusts most officer training to senior non-commissioned officers (SNCOs). They become the most influential people in your life. They make you angry, dejected, frustrated and tired. They also make you listen, laugh and learn. Only the best become instructors, usually after ten to 15 years of service. Each of the seven platoons in our intake had a colour sergeant or staff sergeant. For them, it can be a career highlight; they've started from the bottom and are now training future leaders. For us, it became a love-hate relationship. We loved to hate them when things were shit. Equally, we hated that we loved them. Because, for the period at Sandhurst, they provide a handrail, a source of information and advice. Sandhurst Stockholm Syndrome. We each craved the approval of our instructors while resenting them, and ourselves, for craving it.

Phase one training for non-commissioned soldiers – i.e. non-Sandhurst and non-officer training – lasts 14 weeks. In that period, you are taught to march, shoot, move tactically and patrol. At the same time, you learn discipline, time management, organisation, how to deliver orders and teamwork. Put simply, those 14 weeks are when civilians become soldiers. Officer training at Sandhurst is different. Instead of 14 weeks, it lasts 44 weeks. In addition, that 14-week civilian-to-soldier phase is compressed into an all-consuming, exhausting and notoriously sleep-deprived first five weeks with a training schedule comfortably tipping over the 100-hour-per-week mark.

That first day went by in a blur. We walked as a group – vaguely in step and vaguely together – to different places around camp. Before we moved anywhere, we did a number check. Each number was called out quickly and clearly. It was an easy way to assure the group that each of us was there.

Whilst we picked up more kit, various other places of interest were pointed out: the medical centre, gym, parade square, remembrance chapel, athletics track and NAAFI (Navy, Army and Air Force Institutes). There's a NAAFI on every military base. It's a welfare place usually containing a small convenience store, a coffee shop and, in the case of Sandhurst, a barber. The latter provided a physical transformation Colour Sergeant Campbell greatly enjoyed as the clippers came out and a standard Army-issue short back and sides was given to all. Soon after, we had our official photos taken and were given our MOD90 – our British Army ID – with our name, height, Army number and rank.

As our group moved around camp, other cadets in uniform were marching together, bracing up – a form of acknowledgement for senior-ranking personnel that are not commissioned officers – and saluting. In the Army, you salute with an open palm facing outwards. It is done as a mark of recognition of the

Queen's Commission – which is awarded to all officers – and for their seniority of rank. This is why, regardless of your personal sentiments towards a senior officer, you salute the rank not the person.

They had different-coloured name tags. They had Sandhurst berets on. Their boots were polished and their trousers creased. They looked smart and assured; whereas we looked a shambles in coveralls and trainers. I felt like the new kid at school in the wrong uniform, unsure of what or where anything was. Thankfully, I wasn't alone.

Having returned to the block, we went for a quick scoff before Colour Sergeant Campbell got us to the line and we settled down again with legs outstretched on either side of the corridor. The first thing he said was, 'Gents, those cadets yous saw earlier – ignore them. Six months ago, they were in the same position as yous are now. You'll get to their level. In fact, you'll be better than them. Trust me, gents.' Each of us, especially the military virgins, breathed an internal sigh of relief.

I got back to my room and looked at the three black kitbags still lying on my floor. I wished I had unpacked them the night before.

⌑ — ⌑

'MAGAZINES! He's checking magazines!' At 0730 on day four, each of us stood outside our identically laid-out rooms awaiting Colour Sergeant Campbell. The message was passed from one corridor to the next. It meant that some poor sacrificial lamb had been caught and the rest of us could learn from his mistakes. While Colour Sergeant Campbell was in someone else's room, we had just enough time to dive into ours and amend an obvious fault.

Yesterday it was dust. Russell had been 'idle' in his approach to the cleanliness of his floor and was subsequently awarded a 'show parade' at 9 p.m. – 2100 hours – outside the guardroom. The rest of us, learning from Russell, were meanwhile on our hands and knees brushing our carpets to make them, in the words of Colour Sergeant Campbell, 'clean enough to eat my dinner off'.

The show parade is another of Sandhurst's peculiarities. The crime committed could be anything: unsecured kit, incorrect haircut, no neck shave, no normal shave, un-waterproofed note-book, unlabelled water bottle, missing Army ID, being early, being late, fluff on clothing or misaligned toothpaste. It could also be for being too tall, too short, too slow, too fast, too cheeky, too boring, having too strong an accent or no accent.

A show parade meant that at 2100 you had to be on the parade square alongside other offenders showing a correction for your error. It could be simple: a labelled notebook if previously unla-belled. Or more elaborate: a video showing you locking your door if you'd been caught with it unlocked, or a photo of your clean sink if it had been found dirty.

Our room inspection wasn't close to being the start of the morning. We'd been up at 0600 to sing the national anthem and drink our bottles of water, having numbered off 1 to 30 with our toes against the line. This time we sang the Armenian national anthem out of respect for our Armenian foreign cadet, Mardirossoyan. Then it was 'block jobs' – scrubbing the floors, cleaning the loos, dusting the corners of the corri-dors and polishing the door handles. Then a rushed breakfast at 0700 before tidying our rooms for inspection at 0730 in combats.

At 0730 today, the emphasis was on our dirty magazines. By dirty magazines, I mean an unclean ammunition storage and feeding device. Explaining to my parents that a short Glaswegian man was punishing me for having dirty magazines by my bed was indicative of my lack of perspective.

We knew how it worked with rifle magazines. Clean the outside of them – make them look sparkling – and you'll live to fight another day. But not today. Today, Colour Sergeant Campbell wanted to dismantle them and inspect them for interior rust on the springs. With so many other lines of attack to counter, nobody had anticipated this.

'Good morning, Colour Sergeant. 30158227, Officer Cadet Stewart, awaiting your inspection.'

'Good morning, Mr Stewart. And what a beautiful morning it is, too. I wouldn't want to be anywhere else. How about you, Mr Stewart, anywhere else you'd rather be?'

I began to think of Michael Palin's Monty Python sketch about soldiers on parade admitting to their instructor places they'd rather be. There were many places I would rather have been than standing at attention outside my room at 7.30 a.m. awaiting an inspection from a quick-witted Glaswegian with a sharp eye. 'Absolutely not, Colour Sergeant.'

'I hoped as much, Mr Stewart. Here at the *finest* military academy in the world.' He often placed emphasis on the word 'finest'. 'So, let's see what we have inside and whether it's an improvement from yesterday. As we both know, that was… poor.'

Colour Sergeant Campbell had two gradings for performance: poor and satisfactory. Even when the result was clearly impressive, he would say, 'Gents, that was… satisfactory.' Yesterday, a significant proportion of the contents of my room – namely my sheet, duvet and pillows – had been tossed out the window when it failed to meet Colour Sergeant Campbell's standards. Today was a new day, though. A new start, perhaps.

He sauntered into my room and surveyed the scene before peering wistfully out the window. He neglected to mention the parachuting lesson my bedding had been given yesterday and seemed uninterested in the state of my magazines. Instead, he turned around and opened my cupboard.

'Please identify that, Mr Stewart?'

'What, Colour Sergeant?'

'That, Mr Stewart.' He pointed into the cupboard.

'That's a dead fly, Colour Sergeant.'

'That's two show parades, Mr Stewart.'

'What for, Colour Sergeant?'

'Well, Mr Stewart, the first is for having a pet in the grounds of the Royal Military Academy Sandhurst.'

'And the second, Colour Sergeant?'

'The second, Mr Stewart, is for not feeding it.'

And that was that, another inspection and another morning at the finest military academy in the world.

After room inspections, the day began proper at 0830 with a 90-minute Physical Training (PT) class, a quick change back into combats for a two-hour rifle lesson before an ethical warfare presentation. Lunch was at 1300, a quick scoff of carbs on carbs on carbs – pasta, chips and a jacket potato being a common combination; this was followed by a two-hour signals lesson. At breakneck tempo we marched from our signals lesson to drill lesson at 1600 in a different order of dress. Somebody along the line invariably forgot something, went to wrong location or was wearing the incorrect clothing.

It was 1605. We were late. Colour Sergeant Campbell wasn't happy.

'Gents, timings are critical, not optional!'

He was impeccably dressed in a pressed kilt and tartan sash. 'Gents, where are your water bottles?' We rushed upstairs to grab them, filled them to the brim, checked our surnames were correctly stencilled on the green tape on the outside of the plastic one-litre canteens and reformed as a platoon.

With fresh blisters and cracks in the polish on our boots, drill finally ended. We changed back into combats again and headed down for dinner which was another multiple-carb plateful. We returned to the lines and, finally, had time alone in our rooms.

I texted Sophie for the first time that day and asked if she would be free for a call in five minutes. I took off my boots, set up my ironing board, changed into my tracksuit and clicked 'video call'. There wasn't time in the day for phone conversations without some 'concurrent activity', as Colour Sergeant Campbell referred to it, but Sophie was used to me ironing or polishing as we spoke. Just as she was explaining how her family were doing, I heard those bloody three words being passed from one corridor to the next: 'On the line!'

'I'm sorry, darling, got to go. Speak in a bit.'

Colour Sergeant Campbell was there outside his office in his tracksuit. The 30 of us lined up and numbered off. Our enunciation reflected our evident lack of enthusiasm.

'Gents, take a seat.'

After a day of being bounced from pillar to post, being told to take a seat should have been a positive. In reality, it meant another lesson. Not an official one but a 41 Platoon special. These had their pros: informal, informative and relevant; and their cons: time-consuming and long-winded. When all we wanted to do was be left alone, speak to our loved ones, prepare for the next day and sleep, these 'quick wee chats' were a mixed blessing.

Colour Sergeant Campbell spoke of his time in training, mistakes he'd made and things he wished he'd known if he had his time again. It was his way of imparting wisdom in a less trans-actional and more transformational manner. With that finished, we looked at the training schedule for tomorrow before going to our rooms and finally shutting the door on another day.

I texted Sophie, 'Sorry, colour sergeant wanted to chat to us. You still up? Speak in 5?' I flicked the switch to warm up my iron, filled the water tank, laid out my combat trousers and clicked 'video call'. It was reassuring, pleasing and 'normal' to see her face again – a break from Sandhurst. I ironed the front and rear of one trouser leg, then the front and rear of the other. Not creating any tram lines – two creases next to each other – was key. I then moved to my combat shirt, pressing down firmly on the collar and the creases running from the shoulder to the cuff. I rolled back the sleeves to the exact length – four fingers above the elbow – ensuring that left matched right. I then got out my drill boots and applied a layer of black Kiwi shoe polish using a damp Selvyt polishing cloth, then put them to one side while they dried. In the meantime, I brush-polished one layer of brown Kiwi shoe polish onto two different pairs of boots. I added a second layer of black Kiwi boot polish to my drill boots.

As I kept Sophie informed about proceedings at our end and heard about her day at work, I got out my second and third drill shirts and carefully ironed them, then added a quick touch of Brasso to my belt buckle. Sophie told me about her colleagues, and an event they were trying to organise, before saying that she needed to go to bed soon. I apologised again for speaking to her so late and reckoned tomorrow would be better for a proper catch-up. I recalled saying a similar thing the day before. 'Love you,' I said. 'Love you too. Good luck tomorrow.'

The pillow beckoned, but as ever, more was still to be done. I applied a third and final layer of black polish to my drill boots, cleaned the soles of my trainers, used a polishing cloth to make the Brasso disappear and my belt buckle sparkle before re-stencilling my name on green fabric tape to go on my spare water bottle. I put on my flip-flops, edged into the corridor and went for a quick pee. Light was coming from under the doors of every room; each member of 41 Platoon was alone making their preparations for the day ahead. I brushed my teeth and carefully placed my

43

body underneath the taut bedding. My copy of the Sandhurst-issue book, *Serve to Lead,* sat on my bedside table. I opened it up on page six. I read a few lines before my eyes grew heavy and my mind gave up. Maybe tomorrow. I plugged in my phone and set my alarm for 0555. My eyes shut and I went blissfully into the land of nod.

Chapter 3

If the initial stint was the shock of capture, from the sheer intensity and unreality of being thrown into this new state of confinement, then the next phase was the shock of realisation, the dawning awareness that you were in the Army and were being changed by it, for it, bit by uniformed bit. Your actions became subconscious rather than conscious; muscle memory and habits were formed. Although exhausting, the lessons, briefs, lectures, running, marching, ironing, folding, cleaning and brushing became the norm.

Colour Sergeant Campbell's insistent reminders to lock our doors, top up our water bottles and waterproof our notebooks became unthinking actions. We became ironing maestros and proponents of concurrent activity as calls with girlfriends continued to be squeezed within our all-consuming routine. Some, namely Cookson-Smyth, perhaps took concurrent activity a step too far, admitting to having saved time by ironing his uniform whilst wearing it. We began to subconsciously eat, speak and think Army. Even our dreams became part of this existence. Cadets would wake and recount fantasy worlds containing drill, rifle manoeuvres and room inspections. Hours went by in lecture theatres fighting our own inclination towards sleep and watching others lose battles with their eyelids.

Block jobs, inspections, eat, sleep, repeat. It was a simple and repetitive lifestyle. It began with a sleep deprived singsong on the line. It often ended pressing the creases of our drill shirts, aligning our knife, fork and spoon equidistantly on our shelves, folding our socks so that they were smiling and not frowning, re-stencilling labels with a black sharpie or hoovering the carpet. A consistent bit of advice from officers about getting through Sandhurst was to 'Play the game', whatever that meant.

The (not very) secret of basic training *was* playing the game and understanding this was an officer cadet's version of Newton's apple – suddenly things made a bit more sense. In fact, most of Sandhurst was about little apples falling from hidden trees, on unsuspecting heads, all over the place. Stories of cadets sleeping on their floors to protect their beds, or cleaning their rooms in the wee hours, were at once understandable and nonsensical. But self-imposed sleep deprivation to prepare for a room inspection which you were likely to fail, irrespective of the standard attained, was losing. Playing the game correctly meant displaying the right level of caring. Everyone had the same rules but the house – Sandhurst – always won.

'Good morning, Colour Sergeant. 30158227, Officer Cadet Stewart, awaiting your inspection.'

'Good morning, Mr Stewart. And another lovely morning here it is at the *Royal* Military Academy Sandhurst. How are you?' This time, he emphasised the word 'royal'. It somehow added ironic gravitas to our unreal and un-regal surroundings.

'Living the dream, thank you, Colour Sergeant. Yourself?'

'Not bad thanks, Mr Stewart, not bad at all.'

'Mr Stewart, because it *is* such a lovely morning, let's play a game. Pick a number between one and ten.'

'Eight.'

'Right, Mr Stewart, I bet you I can find eight things wrong with your room this morning.'

'I have complete faith in you, Colour Sergeant.'

Like a cheetah browsing the savannah seeking any sign of movement or weakness before launching a fearsome and sudden attack, Colour Sergeant Campbell scanned the room. And then, the cheetah charged. 'One: Blu Tack on wall. Two: dirt on the sole of drill boot. Three: stain on drill gloves. Four: creases on pillowcase. Five: uneven spacing of magazines. Six: inconsistent folding of T-shirts. Seven: lack of polish on drill-hat visor.'

I was as impressed as I was irked by some of the mistakes he spotted. Each morning, every cadet woke with the belief that they might get away with it that day. Why? Because, very occasionally, you did. Very occasionally, the room inspection passed without a correction being issued. Instead, there'd be a 'Mr Stewart, that was… satisfactory.' Two days previously had been one of them. Yesterday had not: Colour Sergeant Campbell had taken an aversion to the height of my books. I was given a show parade for an incorrectly aligned bookshelf.

But the cheetah had been denied. At the crucial moment, Colour Sergeant Campbell had run out of ideas. He had only found seven things wrong with my room. Had the gazelle escaped and survived? I had two options: shut up and take the moral victory, or say something?

'Colour Sergeant, that's only seven.'

He looked right back at me with a glint in his eye. Hook, line and sinker.

'Aye, Mr Stewart, that's only seven.' He'd been holding a tennis ball the entire time. He dropped the ball on the floor. We both watched intently as the bounces got smaller and smaller, until the ball sat motionless and solitary on my carpet in the space between us. We looked up at each other again.

'Number eight: tennis ball on floor. Show parade, showing floor without tennis ball. Have a good day, Mr Stewart.'

Thankfully we had parted company with our coveralls and started donning Army combats. We had been wearing Army-issue Hi-Tec trainers known as 'Silver Shadows'. 'A classic vintage style with a full lace-up front' was how they were marketed. 'Vintage style' sounded reasonable given their Churchill-era design. The same applied for boots: standard issue. With Army combats came another important addition: the beret.

The military beret is an important component of service dress, displayed as official headgear in armed forces around the world. Military berets have been worn in the British Armed Forces since the early 20th century. All members of the British Army wear a beret distinctive to their own unit and regiment. The beret signifies which part of the military you belong to. Over time, the berets of some units have developed their own mystique and history.

For example, in 1918, the British Tank Corps, predecessor to the current Royal Tank Regiment, started to wear a black beret since it did not show oil stains picked up from the interior of the vehicle. Equally, the green beret of the Royal Marines, the beige beret of the Special Air Service (SAS), the maroon beret of the Parachute Regiment and many others have their history and are still worn by soldiers in those units today. In the British Army, the cap badge is required to be over your left eye and the beret pulled down on the right. To achieve individuality within a uniformed organisation, though, soldiers tend to personalise their berets as much as possible through badge location, colour, fade, fluffiness and design.

It turned out that beret moulding was a lesson in itself. We removed the inner lining, shaved the inside and outside before cutting the adjusting string. We dunked them in warm water (not boiling as it causes the wool to shrink) before dunking them in cold water. We placed the Sandhurst cap badge above our left eye and let it dry as we stood topless letting the blue-dyed water trickle down our chests. And then we had to push, pinch, shape, squeeze, tweak, mould and personalise them until they got the okay from Colour Sergeant Campbell.

Beyond hair length, another Army requirement was the shaving of facial hair, with punishment for those caught failing to shave daily. I discovered this early on. Colour Sergeant Campbell was bored on parade and prowled up and down the line, spotting anything and everything from dust to soap suds, from nose hair to dirty laces. He stopped in front of me.

'Mr Stewart, how are we today?'

'Good thanks, Colour Sergeant, how are you?'

'Aye, not too bad, thank you.'

'Mr Stewart, integrity test, have you shaved today?'

Integrity was one of the Army's six core values. When used as a questioning method such as this, it usually meant the questioner was certain of the truth; they were simply testing the moral compass of the soldier in question. Colour Sergeant Campbell knew I hadn't shaved that morning, which left me, in that moment, with a simple choice: either to tell the truth or to lie. Instinct said lie. He would question it. I'd double down. He couldn't prove otherwise, but he'd silently judge me. Short-term win, long-term loss. I weighed the odds.

'No, Colour Sergeant, I haven't.'

Failing to admit was failing this test. But admitting to failing to fulfil a basic soldierly task was a failing also. Regardless, it was another example of the instructors and the system – Sandhurst – winning.

41 Platoon and marching did not coexist peacefully in those first few weeks. Most days, hands and feet moved wildly out of sync.

All over the world, basic military training involves learning to march. Marching is used to display synchronisation and strength as well as building the cohesion and confidence of soldiers. When performed well, it is stylish and organised. The process of attaining this excellence, however, is best kept hidden from the public eye.

None of us were used to walking in a group of 30 in boots that felt like dumbbells, in a hat that was about to fall off and flanked front, rear, left and right by fellow uncoordinated participants. We weren't used to walking while pressing our thumbs downward and forward in a fist as an extension of our arms. We weren't used to having our 'arms shoulder-high', being 'on the heel' or being told to get 'your chin up and your head back'. Even our own colour sergeant's Scottish accent confused us, but we lacked the temerity to say anything. He'd say, 'Brace up!' and what followed could either have been 'Show the movement' or 'Shoulder movement'. To this day, I still don't know the answer.

Each instructor had their own version of left, right, left, right. Colour Sergeant Campbell's sounded more like 'luf, riii, luf, riii', while others had more of a 'lo, rye, lo, rye', or a 'leff, rai, leff, rai'. Meanwhile Colour Sergeant Campbell's most often-heard phrase as we moved around these famous grounds was 'Change step!' – a mechanism to get the platoon in order. He'd give the warning, 'Changing step', so we were prepared for the command of 'Change step!' that followed. At that instant, all the cadets would stop with their left foot stationary and bring their right down at a 45-degree angle behind the left foot. We'd then all march off again in sync. It was like when a computer technician recommends you turn your computer off and then on again to reset the system.

We were often lambasted for tick-tocking. Tick-tocking is an unfortunate error in drill where your right arm and right leg move forwards at the same time. It sounds illogical and unnatural. It's both. But it can and does happen. In practice, some 'lunatic', 'lizard' or 'mutant' (now commonly used terms) almost always mistimed their step and our ragtag bunch advanced akin to a conga line. This solicited a machine-gun-fire barrage of Campbell one-liners as our colour sergeant demanded improvement in the apparently unimprovable.

But march we did: from the signals wing to the block, from the block to PT, from PT to the dining room and from the dining room to the lecture theatre. We always marched.

Slowly but surely, almost to our own amazement, we improved. We achieved a modest proficiency in walking together and standing still. And we were constantly reminded of what a modest skill it was. Enter the company sergeant major (CSM). Both Falklands and Imjin companies had a company sergeant major and a company commander. Together, they oversaw the platoon commanders, colour sergeants and, ultimately, us, the hundred or so officer cadets. Unfortunately for the colour sergeants, this CSM had previously been an instructor at Sandhurst. He knew their job inside out. Unfortunately for us, he had previously been an instructor at Sandhurst *and* a platoon commander in Afghanistan. He also knew our job inside out.

The CSM, aka 'the Bear', was a specimen of Herculean mass. Not as comfortable on the parade square as he was in the field, he nonetheless understood it was part of his job. He was also acutely aware of what drill *should* be and therefore struggled to understand other people's incompetence. His humbling words, 'This is a simple coordination exercise', were invariably followed by, 'It's not rocket science, gentlemen.' To the Bear's way of thinking, our task should have been easily manageable given that, according to him, we graduates all had 'brains the size of small planets'.

As an officer cadet, you were not allowed to go anywhere on camp without marching or running. Yet if you were running, people asked questions. So you marched. Arms shoulder-high, thumbs down, chest out, chin up, head back and mouth shut. Learning to march was about forming habits. Sandhurst's nickname, the 'Factory', was not misplaced: civilians went in, officers came out. Learning drill was another the way the factory belt worked.

Also included among what the Bear referred to as 'Billy Basics' were rifle lessons. And I specifically say rifles, not guns. They're weapons, weapon systems, gats or firearms. One thing they're definitely not are guns; except, oddly, the General Purpose Machine Gun (GPMG). Lessons in the Skill At Arms wing involved highly-strung instructors getting frustrated teaching officer cadets how to handle an SA80 assault rifle. Through Rifle Lessons 1-12, our aim was to learn to safely handle, load, unload, shoot, remedy and clean this intricate device.

Those in the Reserve, graduates of the UOTC and ex-rankers were expected to find Junior term (Juniors) relatively simple. They had already covered much of the basic soldiering content of the course which was new to the rest of us, the military virgins. We would, or rather should, catch up in Intermediate term (Inters) as we all learned new content and encountered new scenarios.

For someone like Naj Abil, who a few months earlier had been roaming the streets of Afghanistan with a pair of pistols and an AK-47 as part of the Afghan Special Forces, an SA80 was relatively simple. For a military virgin such as Norton, it was like handing a Rubik's Cube to a puppy. The monkeys typing Shakespeare comparison came to mind. We knew he'd get there – it was simply a matter of when.

The classrooms were austere and cold with concrete floors and aged posters of crosshairs and snarling silhouetted men. But learning how to handle a gas-operated assault rifle that could fire 5.56-millimetre ammunition a distance of 300 to 400 metres, at a rate of 610–775 rounds per minute, was hardly a soft subject. So we learned to dismantle and reassemble our SA80s. We remembered their weight, capability and potential attachments. We changed magazines efficiently and resolved blockages. We were tested and retested, inside and outside, standing up, on one knee and in the prone position. We went from walking to running, to the prone position to leopard-crawling and back, before words of command changed our process and we'd fire rounds before changing magazines and firing positions. Two rounds and move, two rounds and move. We learned to zero our rifles, take care of them, clean them and oil them. Understanding how an SA80 operated was a fundamental aspect of soldiering. Getting to a stage of genuine competence was a long, stressful and sometimes embarrassing process. It was also necessary and satisfying.

And then there were signals lessons in the adjacent Communication Information Systems (CIS) wing. In the breaks between rifle lessons, we sat on our hard plastic chairs in a circle and drank water from our black bottles, but the signals wing had a tuck shop – a dangerous temptation for sleep deprived officer cadets. So we stocked up on Haribo to keep us awake without factoring in the sharp energy-level cliff we'd invariably tip off when our blood sugar plummeted.

The signals lessons taught us how to assemble and programme radios as well as communications, signalling and radio logging. We learned the current NATO phonetic alphabet. Delta, Oscar and Tango became engrained in our language; no more fumbling around for David, Orange and Tank while someone else said Donut, Olive and Tulip.

We learned the correct British Army Voice Procedure (VP) saying 'Roger' instead of 'Copy that'. The use of 'Roger' dates to the Second World War. It originates from the practice of telegraphers sending an 'R' to stand for 'received' after successfully getting a message. This was extended into spoken radio during the war, with the 'R' changed to the phonetic alphabet equivalent word 'Roger'. It was coincidental that two-way radio became widespread during the relatively short period when the phonetic name of the letter 'R' was 'Roger'. Before 1940, it was 'Robert', and from 1956 on, it has been 'Romeo'. Had the technology arrived a little bit earlier or later, we might have been saying 'Robert that' or 'Romeo that'.

It was engrained in us how and when to repeat geographic coordinates, how to send long messages, never to swear and never to say 'Over and out', the reason being that the two words have distinct and contradictory meanings. 'Over' is used at the end of a transmission, telling the receiver that the transmitter has finished that section of their broadcast and is awaiting a response. During a conversation, 'over' can be and is likely used on multiple occasions, but 'out' should only be used once as the final word. 'Out' means that the transmitter has finished speaking and is not expecting to hear any more from the receiver – i.e. the conversation is complete.

Within each platoon there was a wide range of skills and experiences. While the importance of radio communication was undeniable, for budding infanteers, understanding the basics was a tedious, but necessary, first step in mastering the cut and thrust of basic soldiering. For others, the signals wing was a much-welcomed cerebral break from the physical intensity of the rest of the course. Everyone at Sandhurst does the same basic training, regardless of whether they'll commission and become a teacher, signaller, engineer or logistician, or go to the Infantry or Royal Armoured Corps (RAC). Everyone needs a proficiency in both radio programming and operating an assault rifle.

Beyond developing specific skills, we were also physically re-engineered to make us stronger, faster and more resilient. We did heavily weighted marches, sprint sessions and circuits. We were conditioned to develop our mental and physical robustness. And the Physical Training Instructors (PTIs) helped get us there.

In the Army, there's a PT Corps, a specific unit dedicated to physical training. In the civilian world, activities such as running, cycling, going to the gym and so on are called 'exercise' or perhaps 'training'. In the Corps, it's 'phys'. Rope climbs: phys. Mountain biking: phys. Athletics: phys. And best of all, as the PTIs take great pains to remind you, it's free. A weighted march in the rain: free phys. A sickening hill sprint session: free phys. Lifting heavy things in the gym and putting them down again: free phys. If it's free and it's phys, PTIs are happy. Well, almost.

Being so focused on phys makes PTIs a different breed. PTIs don't care whether you're straight off exercise, covered in cam cream or sleep deprived. Their only concern is your free phys programme and the clothing you wear. To use political-campaigning language, PTIs have unwavering 'message discipline'.

Regardless of who attended the class, the 41 Platoon PTI, a Welshman by the name of Staff Davies, started each lesson with 'Sirs, ma'ams, ladies and gents'. Following that, Staff Davies, whom we always referred to as 'Staff', asked whether we'd had a proper breakfast, were currently hydrated or had any outstanding injuries, all questions nobody responded to with any integrity.

PTIs haven't always been PTIs – something they often remind you of. They were soldiers once, before their stint in combat uniform came to an end and a new, highly pressed outfit awaited. Their green synthetic T-shirt was replaced by a white cotton vest with red edges. Their green Army belt was replaced by a red one with a shimmering buckle. Their combat trousers were replaced by bleached white shorts with a bullet-straight crease down the front and centre of each side. Their socks are the whitest of white, which would put even the American dental industry to shame, and sit precisely two fingers above the rims of their pristinely white trainers. PTIs tuck their laces in. As life advice, it's recommended not to interrupt a PTI basking in their own reflection.

The purpose of our PTIs was to build in us a strong level of physical capability – and they were bloody good at doing it. PT sessions were consistently and rightfully tough. Low standards weren't accepted, and nor should they have been. Being fit had a disproportionate weighting on your apparent competence as a leader. Being quick mattered more than being strong, and first impressions were shaped by your Personal Fitness Assessment (PFA) performance. The PFA was a standardised test: a constant and inescapable barometer that involved doing as many press-ups as possible in two minutes, followed by as many sit-ups in the same timeframe, followed by a 1.5-mile run.

You hear the horrible lines: 'Press-up position down... Two minutes best effort, standby... GO!' The beady PTIs strut up the line of cadets commenting on flawed technique and reminding us to keep our elbows in. In pairs, we then count our partner's effort before doing two minutes of sit-ups each while being reminded by toned men in tight white clothing to keep our hands in our clavicles and our feet pressed firmly into the floor. For clarity, it sounds more suggestive than it is.

Now Falklands Company are waiting – nervous, tense, twitchy – at the painted white line that says 'PFA START LINE'. The Sandhurst 1.5-mile route hasn't changed in decades. Neither has the PT gear; we each wear a baggy blue or maroon cotton T-shirt. Staff Davies stands with an oversized stopwatch. Everyone knows that, after the following words, the comments end and the pain begins. 'Standby... GO!' The banter stops and the jostling and nudging is underway.

The first 800 metres, downhill and relatively straight, lull you in. As the road bends sharply to the left, you have a split second to glance at who's behind. The road gently rises as the mass of Old College appears on your left. You pass the Queen Victoria statue by your right shoulder, then the canon. The only sound is that of your own breathing, the breathing of those around you and your Silver Shadows hitting the concrete. The course flattens out as New College appears to your left: 1600 metres gone, 800 metres to go. Those who misjudged their efforts by starting too fast are dropping back through the pack now and wishing it would end.

You do a 180-degree hairpin and the end is in sight 400 metres away. You want to stop but you can't. You're compelled to continue because those in front and behind haven't given up. Maybe they're having the same internal conversation. There are 200 metres to go. It's all heart now. A final push and it's over. Finally. You're given a token with a number as you stagger and splutter exhausted, filled with lactic acid and relieved. Within a few minutes you're back outside the gym, being told by the PTIs not to be sick outside 'their' gym before being marched back to the block for a quick shower, a change into combats, a topped-up water bottle and more marching before more rifle lessons. Another afternoon in Junior term complete.

⌒ — ⌒

Basic soldiering is a key component of phase one training. By this, I mean a team of people with rifles in camouflage and cam cream moving stealthily and shooting straight. The classic Army image. For us, this meant heading to the local training area and going 'Into the Field' or going 'On Exercise'. The whole training programme was geared around big exercises, and exercise names were always in CAPITALS: LONG REACH and CRYCHAN'S CHALLENGE in Juniors, FIRST ENCOUNTER and DRUID'S RIDGE in Inters, BROADSWORD and DYNAMIC VICTORY in Senior term (Seniors). There were others but those were the big hitters.

Our first, however, was Exercise SELF RELIANCE, a simple week-long introduction to field soldiering.

Life in the field was putting into practice much of the theory learned in camp. You learn navigation, ground analysis, rifle handling, radio communications, time management, how to receive and deliver orders, discipline, delegation and the principles of war so you can operate effectively. Other than when consciously seeking cover, there's no hiding in the field – it's a magnifying glass on your competence. It was eagerly anticipated by some and dreaded by others. The classic unspoken (but frequently spoken) game of one-upmanship about one's competence in the field was a thread across all ranks and all job roles.

We learned the basics: hand signals and manoeuvring individually, in pairs, as a fireteam, in sections and platoons. Although we were part of a platoon in camp, the structure and dynamics were different in the field. In British Army doctrine, each platoon is split into three sections and each section has a specific role during a platoon attack – usually assault, suppress or reserve. Each section is split between Charlie and Delta fireteams led by the section commander and section second-in-command (2IC).

As ever, the day started with reveille. Pronounced 'r'valley', it's the term used for the time soldiers need to be up in the morning. It comes from the French word *réveiller*, meaning 'to wake up'. Given its peculiarity, Army folk spell it each and every way possible with accents thrown in arbitrarily. This was followed by 'stand-to' for 15 minutes, when everyone faced outwards with our rifles from our 'harbour area', or secure base, in preparation for the enemy's attack. The enemy were not, of course, an actual enemy. They were members of Gurkha Company Sittang – the 'enemy' stationed at Sandhurst. They were full-time soldiers and this was a temporary posting. They would dutifully and periodically fire a few rounds when told over radio and move when they were told to.

Our instructors, also known as Directing Staff, or DS, were on high alert to spot eyelids rather than eyeballs during stand-to. Morning administration then took place; along with the others in our shell scrape ('fox hole' in US Army terminology, 'scratcher' in colour sergeant terminology) we took turns to heat up the boil-in-the-bag food, clean ourselves and our rifles (the latter *should* take priority), shave and put on our Army make-up, i.e. cam cream. Time was at a premium. We weren't in a race but, as ever at Sandhurst, you didn't want to be the last to complete anything.

We learned about Hexi TV, the exhausted, semi-comatose state in which you watched your food cook on an Army stove using hexamine fuel tablets. We learned sentry duty, track plans, how to keep our feet in good order using talcum powder and how to dry them using Gore-Tex socks. And we learned a *lot* of acronyms. How to deliver orders CLAP (Clear, Loud, As an order, with Pauses); CAKE (Concurrent Activity, Anticipation, Knowledge, Efficient Drills); sentry HOTO (Handover-Takeover) procedure. White light was sinful, red light was embraced. Silence was golden. The goal was concealment and covertness – seeing but not being seen. Black, brown and green cam cream was used on your face and hands to break up the colours on your skin. Use of the word 'please' was frowned upon in camp; it was forbidden in the field. Politeness and civility ceased to exist. Functionality, directness and clarity took precedence. Phones, naturally, were left behind.

A few poor military virgins, still 'Hollywoodised', answered on the radio, 'Copy that' rather than 'Roger'. Colour Sergeant Campbell was alert as ever.

'Mr Cookson-Smyth,' he said, 'Just confirm I heard "Copy that"?'

Realisation dawned. Silence.

'Mr Cookson-Smyth...' The name hung.

'Roger, Colour Sergeant.' It wouldn't happen again.

Like paying taxes or washing up, being on stag, or sentry duty, was unpopular but necessary. The person managing the roster had immense power at the tip of their Lumocolour marker pen, which could unwisely be exploited for short-term bliss. They could give themselves the first stag duty, just as everyone else was preparing to 'get their nut down', or go to bed. This meant, post-stag, they were free to gonk (sleep) uninterrupted until stand-to several hours later. No nudge in the night with those horrendous PTSD-inducing words, 'Mate, you're on stag.' When the roster was distributed, self-interest or lack thereof was evident.

On stag, you'd often find yourself in the dark by yourself for an hour, trying to remember a four-letter password given to you, wishing you could have a cigarette, wishing it would stop raining, wishing you were warmer, wishing the seconds would turn to minutes and the minutes to an hour. Basically, wishing you weren't on stag. With ten minutes left of your hour, you'd get up, locate the next beneficiary, give them a gentle nudge and tell them, just as you were told an hour before, 'Mate, you're on stag.' A quick handover would take place: reference points, boundaries, primary and secondary means of communication etc. At this point, your hour was up, your work was done and you'd be free to return to your 'green time machine', your Army-issue sleeping bag.

It is said that officership, leadership even, is doing the right thing, not the easy thing. It was a mantra reiterated perpetually at Sandhurst. Writing the roster and giving yourself the best hour to be on stag was a very small thing. Every day, however, included numerous small tests that entailed choosing the right thing versus the easy thing. Life in the field was an extension of that, almost an exaggeration of the maxim. Each decision to dismantle and clean our rifles, opposed to just adding oil, or allowing our mates into the harbour area when they forgot the entry password, meant a decision about the right thing versus the easy thing.

We were impressed by the professionalism of our instructors and pushed to reach the exacting standards they set. Each 'Mr Stewart, just confirm' encouraged me to think about my actions and empowered me to do the right thing. It was the same for the other cadets. SELF RELIANCE was our first exercise, the least complex, the least tiring and the least memorable, but arguably the most important. It provided the foundation, the building blocks from which our discipline, knowledge and competence would develop.

—

'ON THE LINE!'

For fuck's sake. I'm standing in my towel when the familiar call goes down the corridor. Trackies, T-shirt, flip-flops, go.

'Twenty-seven!'

I get there just in time.

'Right, gents. Three things. Number one: security of kit. Some of you mutants are not locking your doors. Watch out, gents. That's all I'm saying, watch out. Number two: gents, perception is king. Remember that, perception is king. As officers, you need to consider the image you project to those under your command. And number three: values. Each of you will laminate this and put it on the mirror in your room. Every morning and evening when you're brushing your teeth, you will look at this. That's it. See you later. And gents, one more thing. I'm always watching. Remember that.'

We each take our piece of paper, go to our rooms, laminate it and place it in the top right-hand corner of our mirrors. It is a picture of Colour Sergeant Campbell. His pressed uniform, rank slide, name badge and stern expression are clearly on display. Beneath his picture, the message reads:

'My Men

My Weapon

Myself

I am always in command appointment from the minute I wake.'

The motto of Sandhurst is 'Serve to Lead'. Your job as an officer is the care of the soldiers under your command. To lead is to serve those under your command before you serve yourself.

⁊ — ⁊

'Okay, gents, parade square at 0600. Tracksuits.'

'Colour Sergeant, won't it be dark then?'

'Aye, aye, 0600 it is, gents.'

We marched to the parade square in our tracksuits in the dark and went through the upcoming drill test procedure. It was mid-September and, importantly, it was Friday at the end of week five. Pass the drill test, answer a few questions about key Sandhurst staff and we were free for our first long weekend from the Academy.

Tensions rose as we dressed in our ceremonial blues, or No. 1 dress uniform, and checked ourselves and each other over – the 'buddy-buddy system' in Army terminology – to ensure that the person next to us was in good order. Our boots glistened, our heavy woollen outfits were spotless and our creases were pressed.

'Right, gents, this is it. Left, right, left, right. Platoon, platoon… HALT!'

The ground shook as our heels came down. Obviously, it didn't actually but that was one apparent aim; another was to drive your heel through the concrete and smash the Aussies on the crowns of their heads. We were there together, in sync, in step and in time. The Bear's line to Mr Norton – 'Introduce your top lip to your bottom lip' – might have had an impact. The thought occurred that this might be a success.

'Platoon will advance to the left in threes. Left… TURN!' We were all impressed. No mutants getting it wrong this time. We were running on adrenaline and a deep desire to get home. The genuine concern of a reshow had switched our minds into gear.

'By the left, quick MARCH!' And off we went. Heads back, chins up, arms shoulder-high, each man keeping to the heels of the man in front. We did an about-turn, we saluted to the left, then the right. It was good – in time, professional and perhaps even stylish.

I can't recall how exactly but things altered on an 'about turn', a 180-degree direction change. Norton's metal stud hit the concrete and off he went, ass over tit, man down. The parade halted. He stood, stumbled and fell again. He uncomfortably removed himself. The subsequent personnel changes had drastic consequences.

Unprepared and unqualified for this command appointment, another cadet, Patel, was now leading the platoon. He panicked and stepped off on the wrong foot. We all, therefore, did the same, or some of us did. And some was enough for the whole system to fail. Like a slinky going down the stairs, everyone bunched together before stretching out again leaving irregular gaps. Groans followed. We did a left turn but Cookson-Smyth inexplicably turned right. Others followed. There were cadets all over the place, vigorously marching in different directions. Colour Sergeant Campbell had no control and shouted meaningless, incomprehensible commands. Put simply, it was a 'shitshow'.

We were called to a halt. It had started with such promise and ended up not just disappointing, like a band's tepid second album, but laughably bad. With the 30th man now in the med centre being treated for concussion, 29 of us were marched off the square.

Later that day, following a semi-successful and just-good-enough reshow, we were gratefully reunited with our families and girlfriends. The nerves, ill-fitting coveralls and name tags they had left behind five weeks ago had been replaced by smartness, discipline, knowledge and professionalism (minus the drill test) – civilians had indeed become soldiers. Our instructors met my parents and Sophie, and, suddenly, instead of Colour Sergeant Campbell and the CSM, it was Craig and Max. Humanising them with real names was confusing, especially as Craig kept addressing both Dad and me as 'Mr Stewart'. They smiled, laughed and made small talk while I stood uneasily by.

Sophie and I drove to her parents' house in London. I was energetic, excited, liberated. Food was the first point of call and I gratefully saw mountains of it laid in front of me: starter, main course, seconds, pudding, seconds. And drink: gin, beer, wine. Maybe it was time to see friends and get drunk. Maybe it was time to 'reconnect' – Netflix and chill, that kind of thing. I had a bath, a long bath, probably too long. I came out dazed. I hung up the towel and nestled under the heavy, fresh down duvet. It felt so different to the coarse Sandhurst sheets. The soft pillow absorbed my head. Each blink became slightly more protracted until, before I knew it, my eyes shut and into the land of nod I went.

The whole first five weeks had been a blur. It was sudden, immersive, intensive, all-consuming, tiring, stressful, hilarious and chaotic. You barely thought more than a few minutes or hours ahead. You had minimal time to yourself and what was left was spent as efficiently as possible. You ran on empty yet ate more than ever. You were exhausted yet you kept going. You were frustrated at knowing little yet accepted that you couldn't remember everything. It somehow just happened. You focused on the next timing, the next test, the next sleep, the next inspection, the next meal, the next anything. But you couldn't escape where you were. You had to be present in this new 100-mile-per-hour world.

An idea passed from generation to generation is that Sandhurst tries to break you, removing the civilian in you, then builds you up again as a soldier. Sandhurst denies this. Almost everyone denies this. And yet, somehow, the breaking-and-building myth persists, and, despite the rebuttals, there's potentially some truth to it. The official narrative says that the commissioning course is designed to build emotional intelligence plus military understanding, honing your leadership potential. But it's not a year-long attendance course. It's designed to be tough.

I was once told Sandhurst was basically Hogwarts with guns: a community with its own games, principles and dialect far removed from those outside, a world within a world. Here, though, you self-selected; you weren't cherry-picked, but rather chose to serve. This world also had no wands, magic or dragons. Instead of Diagon Alley and Gringotts, it was Amazon and Sports Direct. Just as those outside our walls weren't muggles, we weren't wizards; we were just muddling our way from one day to the next. In fact, it seemed nothing like Hogwarts at all.

Chapter 4

'PUBE IN SINK! Show parade!'

Colour Sergeant Campbell enjoyed this line. Any misplaced hair, regardless of colour or type, or simply any general detritus, was deemed show parade-able. 'Pube on desk, show parade.' 'Pube on curtain, show parade.' You get the gist.

'Mr Stewart, what's twenty-one times a hundred?'

'Two thousand one hundred, Colour Sergeant.'

'That's right, Mr Stewart. Twenty-one hundred! And do you know what happens at twenty-one hundred?'

'I'm confident you're about to tell me, Colour Sergeant.' I knew.

'Twenty-one hundred, Mr Stewart. Show parade, showing sink without pube.'

I'm now on parade with 15 other 'offenders'. It's 2055. I'm in combats with a printed photo of my clean sink. The guys to my right and left are in PT kit and ceremonial blues. Almost everyone is in a different outfit – usually what they were wearing, or were meant to be wearing, at the time the offence took place – and holding a different item of kit: shovels, helmets, socks, pictures, water bottles, magazines, hope and everything in between.

'What you showing tonight, mate?'

'Personality.'

'Again?'

'Campbell said it was still below even the low standards I set myself.'

'Classic. You?'

'PT socks not rolled to two fingers above the tongue of my trainers. You?'

'Waterproofed notebook. He threw it in a puddle to prove my Tesco Ziploc wasn't up to standard at the *Royal* Military Academy Sandhurst.' Philipps could usually be relied upon for an impeccable impression.

Show parades were primarily a punishment. They were also to remind us not to make the same mistake twice, not to take it too seriously and that, whatever we did, Sandhurst would usually win the game and we just had to play to the best of our abilities. It was a nuisance, disrupting an evening and taking up time, your most valuable commodity. Nabbing time was the same reason Colour Sergeant Campbell called out people's names to keep him company as he ironed or polished. 'MR STEWART... let's have a quick wee chat.' He was aware that his 'quick wee chats' ate into our time, invariably leaving us ill-prepared and late for whatever came next. It was about the small daily tests as much as the big ones.

You might wonder why we were there at 2055 instead of 2100. Welcome to the concept of 'five minutes before'. The (perfectly reasonable) theory is that if you're there five minutes before, you can't be late. The reality can differ somewhat.

If, for example, the Old College Commander, a lieutenant colonel, is doing an inspection at 0900, we'd be there five minutes before at 0855 so as not to be late. But five minutes before that, the company commander wants to do his check. Given that's the case, we're there at 0850, so five minutes before five minutes before. But five minutes before the company commander does his check, the platoon commander wants to do his. So we're there at 0845. The colour sergeant wants to check us before that, the platoon duty cadet before that. We also have to check ourselves.

The result is that all 190 officer cadets of CC133 are standing outside in the rain at 0830 in preparation for the inspection at 0900. This is the compounding effect of five minutes before five minutes before. The Old College Commander doesn't see this, though. In fact, he praises us for being on time. We, however, self-assign a commissioning course show parade highlighting a lack of morale, logic and efficient use of resources.

⌐—⌐

It was week six of Junior term and nerves amplified the late-September chill in the air. This was Exercise LONG REACH, a genuine test of resilience, navigation, organisation and teamwork in the Black Mountains in Wales. In a team of eight comprising a range of nationalities, fitness levels and experience, weighed down by heavy bergens (which we now understood to be Army terminology for rucksacks), we had to cover 40 to 50 miles over 36 hours via various checkpoints and command tasks (not seen since the farcical scene of the colonel getting walloped by the knotted rope at AOSB). As a team, we couldn't be more than 50 metres apart throughout.

Across the intake, 24 teams were trying to achieve the same objectives. Not long after sunrise, our team completed our final buddy-buddy checks. Our watches were synced and off we went. With that much distance and time ahead, combined with command tasks and variable weather thrown in, the clusterfuck potential was dangerously high.

Over the hills, into the mist, through the wind and rain, along the ridge, and down. A few command tasks were completed. Before each one we stopped a few hundred metres short, checked each other over, went through the kit checklist (which included two 50-pence coins for use in a payphone in the event of an emergency) and ensured we were in the right frame of mind to tackle the challenge. One involved getting us, our bergens and a few ammo boxes through a spider web-like piece of apparatus while another was to get us and our equipment across a river using a pulley system. All were conducted under a strict time limit. These were simple tasks when performed with full energy in the light of day, but more problematic when fumbling around tired in the rain with minimal visibility.

Then back up into the mist, through the wind and rain, along the ridge, and down again we went. The unspoken bond between us and the grand old Duke of York was by now well established. More command tasks – casualty evacuation along some balancing beams and a wall crossing – and more hills lay in wait. Five miles, ten miles, 20 miles. We'd covered more distance than in a marathon. Into the night with head torches, and tensions arose from exhaustion and hunger. We stopped to rest for a few hours, made a cup of tea, shared a few cigarettes, changed clothes, ate and prepared to move again. Every so often we encountered another team emerging out of the mist. We exchanged stories of laughter, confusion and exhaustion before laboriously moving off again. Most were a person down, a checkpoint down, a failed command task down or were out of time. Everyone was at varying degrees of cognitive and physical functioning.

High on a ridge, 37 Platoon from Imjin Company battled the wind and rain for hours, mindlessly following the footsteps of the person in front and hoping the point man – the person leading the patrol – was navigating correctly. His map was misshapen in the gale, his fingers were numb and his eyes were squinting as the liquid pellets drove into him. He felt a heavy responsibility as the six others (one had already been evacuated) moved zombie-like in silence with their heads down, not knowing where they were. For the best part of three hours, he did what he needed to do when others couldn't or wouldn't; then he got them to the path to take them down off the ridge, out of the wind and below the cloud line. As soon as that path was reached, he upped sticks and moved to the back of the line. He then morphed into zombie mode quicker than an extra in Michael Jackson's *Thriller* video.

To a group of people who were weary and hungry, being led down a path that zigzagged illogically, with decision-making that seemed to prioritise short-term gains, seemed unappealing. 'What if?... ' they tentatively asked each other, 'what if we take off our bergens, lie on them and ride them down the mountain?' The seed was planted. 'You know what, that's not a bad idea.' The herd of unthinking sheep nodded. 'It's quite damp so they'll slide. Our own platoon bobsled team.' And so, at the top of the ridge, the team of seven descended on their bergens. Two went head-first, two legs first, one sat down in a pose of meditative calm and two tried to join their bergens and straddle their legs, as with a bobsled. The ground was moist from the mist and the early phase was smooth. Their descent was rapid as they hurtled downhill. This group of seven were winning the game; they were joyously beating the system as they picked up momentum.

The situation changed as the smooth slope deteriorated and the slick grass became interspersed with gravel and rocks. The team's forward-facing positions began to twist as the bergens redefined their own descending narratives. The seven of them were spinning like saucers, contorting their bodies as they sought to maintain a semblance of control. With a bit of tumbling, rolling and ripped clothing, most made it down. The two bobsledders, credit to them, kept hold of each other and their bergens throughout, providing a justified reason to celebrate. The sitter's body position, lethargy and weight balance were such that, halfway down the slope, he and his bergen disconnected. This was no conscious uncoupling though; more a train carriage being ripped from its engine post-collision. He reached the other six on his arse and chest, arriving ripped and raw. His bergen remained *in situ*.

They all reascended on a recovery mission, bergens removed to save time, located the missing one and smugly trotted back to the bottom. Six of them found their bergens. The seventh, the one who had led them across the ridge and was thus inevitably destined for Sandhurst stardom, went silent. He didn't respond when asked why he was walking in circles in the grass scanning the ground. He finally confessed to having lost his bergen. The group search began. They fanned out and methodically retraced their steps. Nothing. They eventually called it quits until sunrise and collapsed in a lethargic state.

As the Welsh sun peeked its head through the mist, they tried again but lost their bearings and may as well have been searching for the Pennines. The only navigationally competent person was in a tailspin as his glistening military career hung by a thread. All concerns about victory were out the window. The rain fell again. The hope that sunrise had brought was sapped from their broken souls. Begrudgingly our former hero called a halt to the search. Tails between their legs and six bergens between the seven of them, they marked the spot on their map with an 'X', headed towards the nearest checkpoint and confessed their sin to a waiting colour sergeant. And with that admission, a Sandhurst narrative was shaped, to be told, re-told, spliced and spiced.

There was no fanfare, clapping or finishing banner as we crossed the line with a few minutes to spare. There were no social media posts or retweets either. The destination was important, of course, but the journey to get there mattered more. Saying that, the joy of showering, airing our damp feet and blissfully sleeping after a successful completion was hard to beat.

Particular credit must go to Mardirossoyan – or 'Mardy', as we called him – who'd come to Sandhurst from Armenia with limited English and even less understanding of the military. As we had run about like headless chickens in our first few weeks of training – 'flapping' is the Army term for it – Mardy had just smiled obliviously and done as he was told. He was always there, give or take a few minutes and a few missing bits of kit.

Come the 30-mile point of this exercise, Mardy's face reflected a state of perpetual shell-shocked discomfort. He was carrying the shell of a bergen with the contents emptied and shared amongst the team. If we were in pain, Mardy was in more. We fed him painkillers and ibuprofen alongside water, isotonic drinks, flap-jacks and chocolate. He could have called it quits. Yet on he moved like an apocalypse survivor, unsure about each step but somehow tentatively edging forwards to the finish line.

In a post-exercise debrief back at Sandhurst, the chief instructor asked us to tell the most ridiculous stories from each team. Of course, the bobsled team stood out, but there were many others. Some had lost bergens, maps or backbones. Some had gone out of bounds and been intercepted by the commandant. Some had shat themselves, twisted an ankle or been recovered by an ambulance. Some had mouthed off at senior members of staff whom they'd failed to recognise in the darkness. No team had completed all the command tasks and very few had managed to come in on time with a full roster. Only one team had attained the gold medal standard for their performance. The shared expe-riences, hardship, laughter and absurdity were both meaningless and meaningful.

Every officer has their own LONG REACH story of their 36 hours in the Black Mountains. One key takeaway, and joy, from LONG REACH was that you succeeded or failed as a team. If one member failed to continue, the whole team lost. If you stayed together, worked together, shared the weight, painkillers, food, expertise and responsibilities, you stood a chance. The whole thing was very Army: understated, challenging, collaborative and character-building. 'Never again' was the general attitude but that was matched with pride at having given it our best shot and learned valuable lessons along the way.

⌒⁀⌒

Today is a big one for the Sandhurst head honchos. There is an accepted flapping period when a member of high command visits. This agitation is heightened for the visit of Nobel Prize-winning Myanmar politician, Aung San Suu Kyi. Sandhurst is about to be in the media spotlight, hopefully for the right reasons. Suu Kyi is expected to praise the military and the selflessness of its soldiers. She will speak to cadets and instructors before delivering a speech. The visit will present the best of the Army, the historic surroundings and its potential future leaders. Colour Sergeant Campbell says, 'Every man and his dog will be watching.' This means that the swan needs to glide smoothly along the surface while the frantic legs are hidden below.

The visit is planned with, dare I say, military efficiency. The locations, timings, personnel and photo opportunities will be faultlessly curated and executed. Professional sportsmen and women are told by sports psychologists to control the controllables and minimise outside distractions. Sandhurst adopts a similar approach, except it also likes to control the uncontrollables.

It's autumn and we're in week eight. The wind is blowing and the leaves are falling from the trees. It has been this way for the past week, violent gusts sweeping these colourful additions across the bland tarmac of the parade square. But come sunshine or rain, heat or cold, as per unspoken soldiering rules, we keep on keeping on. As the Bear would say, 'The enemy doesn't care if you're wet, cold, tired or hungry.' Wind, rain and wet leaves have caused no disruption to our training schedules. Training schedules don't matter as much as Aung San Suu Kyi, however.

The call came as we were getting changed after a PT session.

'On the Line!'

Colour Sergeant Campbell was standing in the corridor.

'Right, gents, as you know, there's a VVIP tomorrow and we need the place to be gleaming. I need you to go outside and start collecting leaves. The bin bags are here. Fill up as many bags as you can and move them to the guardroom. 41 Platoon, you have been tasked with the pathway and yard. Questions?'

'Just to confirm, Colour Sergeant, we're being asked to hand-pick leaves in the dark when it's blowing a gale?'

'Aye, that's correct.'

And so, just like that, all the officer cadets at Sandhurst put on their tracksuits and gloves, clipped on their head torches and trudged outside with a stack of bin liners to begin collecting leaves.

Brooms were a rarity, maybe one per platoon. For everyone else, you were either a bag holder or a collector of handfuls of leaves. One bag at a time was filled up, tied at the top and moved to the guardroom. We went onto a roster to slip into dinner for additional carbs before going back outside again. Diligently and laboriously, we continued to fill our bags until they ran out, which they did, due to unprecedented demand. We then took to moving the leaves from point A to point B and hoping the leaves would obey the orders we gave them to stay put, just as we obeyed our orders to keep moving them.

The evenings in camp were a time for personal admin – laundry, ironing, polishing, brushing – but also, crucially, the only time to speak to loved ones. I texted Sophie, 'Sorry, darling, can't talk tonight. Stupid tasking. Will explain. Speak tomorrow. Xx' That sort of message had become normal. I was not alone in sending such messages.

'Gents, keep it up. I'll let you know when the situation changes.' Not for the first time, I had to respect Colour Sergeant Campbell. He had told us to prioritise the men under our command from the moment we woke up, and he did the same. He knew it was absurd. But he remained professional and tried to keep our morale up. I have little doubt he vocalised his feelings to his chain of command. But somewhere up the chain, the message was halted or ignored. So we continued into the wee hours, sleep deprived and resentful, handful by handful and leaf by leaf.

'Join the Army, they said. Serve your country, they said. Lead soldiers, they said. Serve to Leaf, they said.' We had to laugh, as replacement batteries were sourced to aid our ailing head torches and we moved leaves back to where they'd come from.

Finally, we were relieved of our duty and returned to our rooms before another message: 'Gents, all to meet on the square at 0600 for Op WIDEAWAKE.' Op WIDEAWAKE was another bizarre task: getting us to check the grounds for potential bomb threats. It seemed a daunting responsibility for unprepared, unarmed and untrained sleep-walking officer cadets at six in the morning.

We woke and met on the square at 0600 as instructed. Surrounding us, rustling around our feet and whipping across the grass beyond, were, as expected, those harmless, colourful, beautiful little things. Everywhere.

We checked for bombs, ate breakfast, polished our door handles, colour coordinated our cupboards and correctly manipulated the morale of our socks. We then conducted Rifle Lesson Five, marched to the lecture theatre and listened to Aung San Suu Kyi's talk about selflessness, kindness and leadership. She seemed unbothered by the beautiful autumnal leaves surrounding the historic buildings. *Thank you very much*, we thought, *for another game of Army.*

As the course moved on, our knowledge increased and part of that was through language and wider Army culture. We understood the difference between OC (officer in charge of something but also your company commander: a major) versus CO (commanding officer: a lieutenant colonel). Sorting something became squaring it away, being in charge became IC, second-in-command became 2IC, For Your Information (FYI) became Situational Awareness (SA), asking someone for an update became SitRep (Situation Report), projected arrival time was Estimated Time of Arrival (ETA) and it was Voice Procedure (VP) for radio communications.

We also learned about wider Army identity and expected behaviours. Corporate companies have leadership principles; the Army has values and standards. These were delivered in formal and informal lectures by our platoon commander, the company commander, the adjutant, the college commander and the padre. A padre is an Army chaplain, of which there are around 150 serving regularly in the British Army. They are unique within the British Army in that they do not carry arms. They're often jokingly referred to as 'Haribo dispensers', given their proclivity to pitch up on exercise and give soldiers Haribo sweets, but their role is more usually one of providing moral support, guidance and pastoral care for soldiers. An important part of their teaching role was conveying, and getting us to embody, Army values and standards.

You're told what these are on day one. They're repeated on days ten and 100 and 1000, as well as on many days in between. There are six values: courage, discipline, respect for others, integrity, loyalty and selfless commitment. They are remembered by one of two acronyms: CDRILS or SOLID C. Simply because it was first said by Colour Sergeant Campbell, I adopted CDRILS. The standards are: lawfulness, appropriateness and professionalism.

Ultimately your conduct would be measured against the Service Test: 'Have your actions or behaviour badly affected, or are they likely to affect, the operational effectiveness of your unit?'

In addition to these official expectations, there were the unofficial, less accountable and less formal ones. These were the daily instructor soundbites, the posters in the lines, cubicles and corridors. 'Do the right thing on a difficult day when nobody's watching', and 'The standard you walk past is the standard you accept.' Then there were leadership quotes, mostly from Churchill, but also from Field Marshal Slim and Field Marshal Montgomery. Slim's big hitter: 'If I were asked to define leadership, I should say it is the "Projection of Personality". It is the most intensely personal thing in the world, because it is just plain you.' In the red corner, Montgomery: 'Commanders in all grades must have qualities of leadership; they must have initiative; they must have the "drive" to get things done; and they must have the character and ability which will inspire confidence in their subordinates.' These quotes were designed to be motivational, to encourage self-reflection, and to help create the framework for the values Sandhurst wanted to instil in us.

When Colour Sergeant Campbell wanted to give us a personal story, we'd get taken to what he called the 'Tree of Trust'. We'd sit, kneel or crouch, come sunshine or rain, and listen to his insights under a tree conveniently located near the block. It was often him empathising, having heard us natter away in the lines. He'd provide insights based on his 15 years of experience in the Army.

'Respect, gents, it's hard to gain but easy to lose. Remember that. Your soldiers, like me, are always watching. Perception is king.' We mocked the 'Tree of Trust' but we also liked it; it felt subtler than formal Sandhurst classes.

Developing trust, teamwork, empathy and relationships takes time. We lived together 24/7, sat together every lecture, slept next to each other on exercise, often showered together and swept leaves in the dark together. It was intense bonding, far beyond a nine-to-five relationship. There was no hiding in your Sandhurst platoon. You knew who fell asleep in lectures, who struggled at which drill movement, who could impersonate which Sandhurst personalities, who was the fastest, slowest, most irritable and most homesick. Some naturally developed leadership positions while others remained in the shadows. Each person wore a mask of competence during the day but battled their own insecurities, stresses and anxieties in private.

Our identity as 41 Platoon naturally emerged. We wanted to be faster, more efficient and better field operators than other platoons. We believed we had the best instructors, the best foreign cadets and the best banter. Our identity as Falklands Company progressed as we received lectures on battles and first-hand accounts from veterans and visited the Falklands cemetery. We also identified as participants in CC133 and, more fundamentally, as soldiers.

Identifying as soldiers also meant understanding potential threats and the impact they might have. Some of those threats involved chemical, biological, radiological and nuclear (CBRN) warfare, something we would learn far more about in Inters.

But to give us a quick glimpse under the bonnet, to understand the dangers, and as a rite of passage, we apparently needed to enter the gas chamber – a term not widely utilised for obvious reasons. So, in alphabetical order, we lined up in front of a small window-less brick building – three by three by two metres – in full CBRN suits with a gas mask at hand. One at a time, a cadet would hold their breath, close their eyes, walk in, remain inside for about 30 seconds and come out the other side. I heard Simpson back there spluttering and coughing.

'NEXT!'

There was no backing out now. It was like going parachuting with a line of people waiting behind you. The light had turned from red to green. You had to jump; you couldn't refuse. With my mouth shut, I went into the dark brick building. I gradually opened my eyes. Colour Sergeant Campbell was there with a gas mask on and a dim light above him.

'Good morning, Mr Stewart.' His voice sounded muffled through the gas mask. I nodded in acknowledgement. 'State your Army number, name and phone number to me slowly and clearly then you're free to go.' He pointed to the door opposite the one I came in.

I looked at him, lifted my gas mask and said quickly, '30158227, Officer Cadet Stewart, 07521956267.' I headed straight for the exit.

'Sorry, Mr Stewart, I didn't catch the middle bit.' There was a glint in his eyes.

I let out an unintended cough and squinted my eyes as the CS gas sat stagnant in the air. Being anywhere near CS gas without adequate protection is a horrible feeling.

I said again, '30158227, Officer Cadet Stewart, 07521956267' before shutting my mouth and holding my breath.

He finally opened the door and let me out. My eyes stung and tears ran down my cheeks as my face grimaced. I was given a pat on the back and a glug of water by Simpson who had just recovered. It felt like 1,000 onions had been cut before my eyes alongside a consistent hacking cough. A former officer described it as being drowned in Tabasco, which seemed appropriate.

Poor Yarrow was in there for an age and came out with the complexion of Casper the Friendly Ghost albeit with a less cheery demeanour.

Colour Sergeant Campbell stood in front of us as we sat with our water bottles. 'Well done, gents. You won't forget that. Unless you're Mr Yarrow who, it seems, forgets a lot, including his own phone number. Mr Yarrow, have a good day.' The nickname 'Casper' stuck.

⌦ — ⌫

By week ten, we were used to getting 20 press-ups for leaving our magazine pouches open, not polishing our boots, having fluff on our berets or not fastening the clips on our daysacks. A daysack is another Army rucksack but smaller than a bergen. And to my knowledge, there's no such thing as a nightsack and nobody knows the answer to 'What's the name of a daysack at night?' We grew accustomed to having the straps on either side of our helmet yanked tight and being called 'Droopy' if we didn't fasten them properly. Similarly, we knew and accepted that leaving our room unlocked would result in it being upturned and our clothes and bedding thrown out the window.

And then there was the visit to Brookwood Military Cemetery. It is the largest Commonwealth war cemetery in the United Kingdom, covering approximately thirty-seven acres. The company got a bus there and we were given a quick brief by the adjutant. He reminded us that being officers, being soldiers, was not the same as being a civilian. Wearing uniform meant something important, something intangible, that couldn't be understood by others. The uniform meant sacrifice. Not just time away from family and friends around the world; not the weekends on duty or Christmases on tour. It meant the contract of unlimited liability; the contract that you need to be willing and able to kill just as you need to accept the risk to your own life. Serving in uniform meant being able to make the ultimate sacrifice.

We were encouraged to walk amongst the graves and be curious about the names, regiments, ranks, ages and words of the dead. Despite us only being a few months into our Army careers and lowly ranking officer cadets, it provided food for thought. So many of the ranks – privates, lance corporals, second lieutenants, captains – had been younger than we were now. Before joining the Army, I had the idea that those who died in war were older people; it made their loss feel less relatable. Walking through Brookwood cemetery this day, I began to realise that every soldier had their own story, life and family; their own loving parents who had a lost a son or daughter, a wife who had a lost a husband, a husband now without a wife or a child who would never feel that warm embrace from their parent again. And many had been young, 18 or 19 years old. You thought of how it had happened. You hoped it had been quick and painless. You hoped they had made a difference, that their deaths mattered.

The days and weeks that followed felt more introspective and the training more pertinent. It was still Sandhurst and still farcical, so we continued to polish our door handles, iron our duvets and ensure our books were aligned. But the trip to the cemetery made us think, as did our initial visit to the Sandhurst chapel with the padre. The chapel is a memorial to commissioned officers who have lost their lives in conflicts around the world. More than three thousand names are inscribed on the pillars inside. In addition, the Book of Remembrance, in the central nave, records the names of almost twenty thousand officers from across the Commonwealth who gave their lives during the Second World War.

Above the arch on the inside of the chapel are the words '*Dulce et decorum est pro patria mori.*' Taken from the *Odes* of the Roman poet Horace, they translate as 'It is sweet and fitting to die for one's country.'

We had group discussions with our commanders. Questions about honour, sacrifice, nobility and service kept surfacing. What would *we* do? What lengths were *we* willing to go to in order to protect our soldiers? What level of sacrifice would *we* be prepared to make for our country? *Was* it sweet and fitting to die for your country in another country thousands of miles from home? Why was *I* wearing this uniform and making this commitment?

These were important thoughts. We shot targets in the morning from ranges of 50 to 400 metres with an SA80 assault rifle from a range of firing positions before applying Asherman chest seals and first aid dressings to gunshot wounds in the afternoon. We thought about bullets hitting the enemy and IEDs hitting our friends. What we were being trained to do wasn't just playing soldiers as children or parading in smart uniforms. We were being trained to develop the necessary levels of emotional intelligence, maturity, knowledge and skills to cope in high-pressure situations.

The question of 'why?' was both essential to ask and impossibly difficult to answer. But each of us needed to. We had provided it hundreds of times to friends and family and at AOSB. Some of the headline reasons were expected, such as 'doing my time' or 'serving my country'. There was the pressure of five generations who had served before, the desire to emulate, perhaps exceed, or merely gain the respect of, high-ranking parents still serving. There was the desire to grow up and to test yourself in the most testing of situations, to know what you were really like as a person.

Some cadets had grown up adoring guns, tanks and Army uniform. Some were newly single and liberated to pursue their own dreams. Some had gone off the rails in their early twenties or had come from broken homes and wanted structure, purpose and direction in their lives. Some had tried corporate jobs in London and wanted to break free. Some wanted the adventure, sport and fitness. Some wanted camaraderie or to be able to say on their deathbed that they had 'done their bit', much as British servicemen responded to the question posed in that famous 1915 Savile Lumley poster: 'Daddy, what did YOU do in the Great War?' Some knew hundreds of serving officers, some knew none.

Yet there always seemed to be a missing piece to the puzzle or an unidentified truth, a deeper reason below the surface that made someone commit to service but which maybe couldn't be easily identified in an interview. In an interview in 1923, George Mallory was asked why he wanted to climb Everest and he simply responded, 'Because it's there.' The line caught the public imagination despite him having answered the question differently on so many other occasions. There's something indefinable about 'Because it's there', something that persuades the human psyche to act in a particular way when logic might suggest otherwise. There are many reasons that divert people away from service to their country, but something had made us, cadet officers of CC133, step forward rather than back away.

Beyond the stereotypes and labels, the reasons are less neat, less ordered. The nuances, the intricacies of why people choose to serve their country and commit to that contract of unlimited liability are usually unseen and unheard, but they're unique and must be sufficient for that person to stay committed and to get through it.

Not everybody who began CC133 on Ironing Board Sunday was going to commission 44 weeks later. The course would continue; the train was rolling and the question was whether you wanted to stay aboard. Physically, mentally and emotionally, some coped better than others. One cadet, McKay, was kicked off the course for inappropriate remarks and an attitude unbefitting of an officer; he failed the Service Test and would soon be a civilian again. His departure reminded us of certain expectations regarding our treatment of others and behaviour in uniform. Moonside, the youngest in the platoon and intake, picked up an unfortunate knee injury on LONG REACH. He tried to keep going but started to miss too much PT. He had to go to Lucknow Platoon and rejoin the next intake at the same stage he left.

Lucknow, Sandhurst's rehabilitation platoon, was where nobody wanted to end up. It either meant your body had been broken and you needed rehabilitation, or you were not at the standard you should be and required additional training before rejoining the course, usually at the same stage you left but with another platoon in a different intake. This was known as being 'backtermed'.

Davis's situation was different. He was amiable, kind and good-humoured. He was on the winning LONG REACH team. He had done UOTC and his dad was in the Army. Coming to Sandhurst was not a decision he went into blindly. But visiting Brookwood made him think more deeply. He realised, perhaps like several others, that being a frontline soldier was not right for him. He then questioned whether he should be part of any of it. Our instructors attempted to keep him but, ten weeks into Junior term, he placed his ironing board under his arm, packed up his car, handed in his Army ID and drove away from Sandhurst.

Colour Sergeant Campbell was disappointed not to see the whole platoon through from start to finish. But he also took a perverse pleasure in calling me into his office, getting out his permanent marker and crossing out the faces of those who would not be continuing on his 41 Platoon team sheet. 'I've always wanted to do that, Mr Stewart. You planning on joining them?'

'I don't intend to, Colour Sergeant.'

'Aye, Mr Stewart. Sink or swim.'

Some believed, as Campbell said, that Sandhurst was sink or swim. It was meant to be demanding, to test your character and force inward reflection. Some felt more could and should have been done to coax cadets through the course, that you're only as strong as the weakest members of the platoon and the aim was to build them up rather than set an unachievably high bar to aspire towards. Others were grateful it wasn't them; that not quitting was a matter of pride rather than staying for the right reasons. Maybe Sandhurst was designed to break you and then build you up again. Or maybe it was designed to break those who were not suited to last the course, and three months into our stint as officer cadets, we had lost three from the platoon. As it stood, the 27 of us who remained were as yet unbroken. It was still to be seen how much building up was to take place thereafter.

Chapter 5

'Where there's water, there's cover, Mr Stewart.'

It was week thirteen and we were on the insertion Tactical Advance to Battle (TAB) for a week-long, sub-zero deployment in the Brecon Beacons in South Wales. Tabbing meant marching loaded with bergens on backs and rifles in hands and this was the start of Exercise CRYCHAN'S CHALLENGE. We each had a spare set of trousers, a couple of spare socks and no spare boots. It was daytime and no suspected enemy were nearby.

Getting to Brecon was its own journey. The night before was spent panicking, packing, unpacking and re-packing. CRYCHAN'S was a tough exercise aimed at conventional warfighting, offensive operations and infanteering. It was designed to test our soldiering ability taught thus far in Juniors, and promised to be a relentless week of battle planning, patrolling and fighting. We and our kit had to be prepared.

As in my first week, I went to the bathroom after midnight and most people's lights were still showing under their doors; each cadet making their own last-minute alterations to their kit, daysack or TAM. A TAM, or Tactical Aid Memoire, is like an individualised Army-specific Filofax. They're Army-issue with an immense amount of information and designed to assist in battle planning and delivering orders. With experience and time, each person tweaks, adjusts and labels their TAM based on their own preferences.

Everyone was likely stencilling, laminating and waterproofing, repositioning their ration packs in their bergens or readjusting the layout of their webbing. These were the small important things, the critical non-essentials. A wet sock leads to chafing which leads to a blister which makes you combat ineffective. A mislabelled water bottle leads to a mistaken bottle mix-up which leads to a poorly supplied patrol which leads to a combat-ineffective soldier. Contingency plan after contingency plan.

She was asleep already but sometime after midnight I texted Sophie to say goodnight and that I loved her. I then set my alarm for 0300. Our bergens had to be loaded at 0330.

An early breakfast followed before we signed out our rifles from a lance corporal displeased by his early wake-up. Unamused by our comments reminding him that he was going back to bed while we were off to Brecon, he made us queue even longer.

We then hopped on the bus and slept, all of us utilising our final opportunity to gonk for gold. Over the bridge and into Wales we went without batting an eyelid. Then it happened: we took a sharp right turn, went over a small bridge and heard the rumbling of the wheels over the infamous Brecon cattle grid. I had never been to this training area before, but that cattle grid was regularly spoken about and the groans from those in the know suggested that it was almost game time. Duvets and showers were out, doss bags and ration packs were in.

We got off the bus and put on cam cream, helmets and webbing. We loaded our four magazines with 30 rounds each, put one in the rifle and three in our front left pouch. The colour sergeants were irritated already that we weren't moving fast enough. They tried to get us 'sparking' by telling us to 'cut around'.

If you're told to 'cut around', it means you're moving sluggishly. Or, in the words of Colour Sergeant O'Sullivan, you're being 'shagging idle'. It often means the shouter is under time pressure, being watched and/or is unsure exactly of what needs to be done, by what method and by what time. The default response: nonsensical bellowing.

Regardless, we cut and sparked enough to progress. The poor sod in charge, Philipps, took a compass bearing and directed his point man, me, forwards to hug a wood line. I could hear the crunch under each of my boots as the December frost was yet to lift from the Welsh hills. And then, without warning, lurking by my right shoulder, the Irish Guards platoon sergeant for 40 Platoon, Colour O'Sullivan, decided to change the situation.

Colour O'Sullivan – he preferred that to Colour Sergeant and I wasn't planning to disagree – ate, drank, thought and dreamt Army. His drill was impeccable, his rigidity in the field terrifying. The way he described the use of a bayonet and driving those seven inches of steel into the sternum of the enemy was alarming. We were never quite sure when he was joking. In the field, Colour O'Sullivan had an unwavering belief that the enemy was watching. He saw the enemy as a God-like presence: omniscient and omnipotent.

I chose to not fully comprehend what he meant by his 'Where there's water, there's cover, Mr Stewart' comment. Of course, I knew what he meant, though, and he knew I knew. I knew he knew I knew. He also knew I'd heard him. He continued to make his point. 'The enemy doesn't give a flying fuck if you get wet. NOW GET IN THAT FUCKING STREAM AND STAY LOW!' I listened, crouched *near* the stream and shuffled along. I was satisfied with my level of discretion. Those behind me were as well.

'WAR ISN'T EASY! IF IT WAS, ANY FUCKING CIVVY WOULD DO IT! SKIN IS WATERPOOF, MR STEWART. NOW GET IN THE DRINK!'

And that was that. Thirty minutes in and I was cold, wet and miserable. We would all remain in a version of that state for the ensuing week.

⌐ ⁓ ⌐

We established a harbour area by 'occupying' a woodblock. The Army calls any sort of wood or forested area a 'woodblock' for reasons I never fully understood. Its density meant minimal light filtered through. From about 1700, we began the night routine of posting sentries. Personal administration had to be conducted by sound and feel alone to maintain light discipline. Not even red light was permitted.

Given the quick change in setting and ambient light, our platoon administration left something to be desired and it was a blessing nobody could see us all fumbling around in our shell scrapes getting ready.

Brecon in December is a tough place to soldier in. Cold, wet and windy, winter in Brecon reminds you that someone is always in a worse position than you – and they're likely on the same exercise. Given my pre-Sandhurst stay in Brecon with Sophie before starting, I had conflicting emotions about this part of Wales. Pre-Army, Brecon was a place of fond memories, quirky pubs and beautiful scenery for me. From now on, I sensed it might always be a little different.

Each platoon had a permanent platoon commander who worked alongside the platoon colour sergeant. In our case, it was Captain Connolly, a Gurkha officer with more than six years' experience in the Army. We knew his presence would develop more in Inters and Seniors and that he'd provide a broader understanding of officership. Throughout this exercise, we'd rotate being acting platoon commander, among other parts we hadn't auditioned for, in a tactical role-playing scenario. Sometimes these lasted an hour, sometimes a day. As DS, Captain Connolly remained with the platoon throughout, oversaw our training, assessed us and gave feedback.

And so proceeded a week of receiving and delivering orders, reconnaissance (recce) patrols and coordinated platoon attacks. One followed by the other followed by the other, all day and all night. It was sunny, then it was rainy, then it was frosty. You sweated when extracting a 90-kilogram cadet on a casualty evacuation, then you sat down alone to write orders. You were the point man on night patrol responsible for the navigation of the platoon before becoming a section 2IC a few hours later. Then you were a radio operator for the platoon commander before becoming a gunner. You were platoon sergeant and then a rifleman. Every role and every attack was different. Hurry up and wait, hurry up and wait, but mainly hurry up.

There are four platoon battle drills: 1. Preparation for battle. 2. Reaction to effective enemy fire. 3. The assault. 4. The reorg (reorganisation). We went through that cycle again and again. As part of phase one, we applied cam cream, drank water, ate something intestine-clogging from our 24-hour ration packs, such as Biscuits Browns or dried raisin and peanut mix, 'bombed' (filled) our magazines and waited.

We now sat in an Army-favoured 'hollow square', the three sections making up the three sides and Captain Connolly, standing with a notebook, making up the fourth.

Something first spotted during the AOSB command tasks countered the widely held perception that all officer cadets want to lead; that by choosing Sandhurst, you've chosen continuous leadership. To dispel that myth further, as Captain Connolly began to issue our command appointments, each of us psychologically shrank. We hoped for pity. We hoped for another role as the grey man, a section 2IC or machine gunner. Maybe a point man if we were feeling bold, or the platoon sergeant's runner. Anything where our heads could safely remain below the parapet. A section commander would be okay, a bit more responsibility but less accountability. Just not a command appointment where success was quickly forgotten and a poorly executed failure forever remembered. In the Sandhurst ratio balancing risk with reward, that was a poisoned chalice.

A few heroes played risky games of 'Brecon Bingo' which took soldierly risk/reward gambling to another level. The rules: pay minimal attention to the orders, take down minimal notes and have minimal situational awareness. The gamble was that you weren't going to be given a command appointment. Anything but platoon commander or sergeant and you'd won, at least that round. Get one of those two, especially the platoon commander role – roughly a 3 to 4 per cent risk – and you've lost… badly.

Sandhurst took no prisoners and neither did Captain Connolly. He loved this game. He revelled in witnessing the trepidation of future leaders wishing not to be assigned additional responsibility. He would delve into his notebook, look around at the blank faces avoiding his gaze and excitedly say, 'Platoon commander, who wants it?' Nobody reacted. Ever. Not a muscle, not an eyebrow raise or even a blink. Not once did anyone indicate even the faintest glimmer of enthusiasm for this responsibility. The wait was agonising; it was the worst wait at Sandhurst. Worse than drill, worse than room inspections, worse than show parades.

About one in five times, Captain Connolly would go with the 'Mr Agnew!' and leave the name to hang in the air, lingering just long enough for him to witness Agnew's personal anguish at the impending assignment. But then, across the frosty ground, Connolly opened his mouth once more. 'Tell Mr Stewart he's the platoon commander.' The briefest of sentences but the words were fateful.

My eyes closed as the realisation set in. The radio was handed over to me along with its three batteries, invariably empty and passed on with the line, 'They were full when I last checked.' They weren't. We both knew it. I signed the dreaded form confirming the transfer of said items and thus accepting financial responsibility if they went missing. I received the platoon commander's daysack (an additional inconvenience seeing as I already had one), another headset (an additional inconvenience seeing as I already had one) and various other accumulated detritus that served to strike additional dread and resentment into the new recipient's mind. And then, just like that, for a period of up to 24 hours, I was in charge of the grateful collective known as 41 Platoon. Having the time of my life as 'Gunner Giveashit' just a few minutes before now felt a lifetime ago. During battle planning, we were often asked to consider the question: has the situation changed? Right now, yes, it very much had.

In command appointment, it was as if the lights were down, the curtains drawn and the solitary spotlight was shining on me. My orders were analysed, my timings checked, my radio communications listened to, my ground awareness scrutinised and my leadership tested. The chances of providing others with fodder for mockery rose exponentially. Navigational mistakes, tactical omissions and pitiful understanding of Army doctrine could all rear their ugly heads at the faintest sight of an enemy position.

Regardless of the DS, one group I couldn't escape was my platoon. They also played the game and you couldn't jack on the person in command appointment. Being 'jack' is basically looking out for yourself, not for others. It is the antithesis of the selfless commitment and teamwork Sandhurst tries to promote. Why? Because it's the right thing to do, because we're a platoon together and because you'd want the same level of effort when the command-appointment roulette wheel spins in your direction. Which it will.

Every command appointment was powered by adrenaline, fear and excitement. There was a terror of doing or saying something wrong, of acting too slowly, or too impulsively, of getting lost or getting embarrassed. Your heart rate increased and not just because of the additional daysack, radio, binoculars and stack of paperwork you've signed but because of the pressure.

Some cadets flipped a switch almost instantaneously and went from being witty, willing and warm-hearted foot soldiers to impatient, irritable and demanding leaders. It wasn't long before the platoon called them out for their personality switches – something usually done in a jovial manner post-exercise but with very genuine sentiments. There were those who only acted with a degree of selflessness when the DS were looking. Despite Colour Sergeant Campbell saying he was always watching, he wasn't. DS watchers were jack whenever the DS weren't watching. They won in the short term, but long-term it usually came back to bite them.

It was time for phase two: reaction to effective enemy fire and the assault. I set a suitable formation, splitting the 27 cadets across the ground, and advanced. The enemy then fired from a distance of 400 to 600 metres – conveniently the approximate effective range of an SA80. Immediately, 'CONTACT FRONT!' was yelled. Everyone went down on their belly buttons. In unison, we all fired blank rounds at the poor Gurkhas under their waterproof shelter. One person shouted using the proper method for an impeccable target indication: 'TWO TIMES ENEMY. CENTRE OF AXIS. FIVE HUNDRED METRES. DELIBERATE FIRE!' There was a difference between 'rapid fire' (30 rounds per minute, i.e. a shot every two seconds) and 'deliberate fire' (ten rounds per minute, i.e. a shot every six seconds).

And then came that brief but essential phase in our 'battle', the moment that could separate a good from a bad leader. My 2IC took over the immediate firefight, while I stepped back to consider the situation: ground, formation, ammunition, enemy position and enemy capability. Then my options: right, left, down the middle, feint, withdraw or encircle. Sandhurst calls this a 'condor moment', one of decision-making serenity and clarity.

In reality, that briefest of moments was internal madness, a cerebral pinball machine. Noises and buzzers were going off, the table was tilting, I was a couple of lifelines down, my left flipper was not responding and a haunting voice from within the machine cackled at my ineptitude.

A few rounds were going off from semi-enthused cadets fighting a thankfully unmoving enemy while I crouched down with a map and determined my course of action. Captain Connolly hovered over my shoulder like a stale fart and made comments such as 'Don't lose the initiative', 'You need to make a decision' and 'What now, Mr Stewart?' My mind was buzzing. My radio wouldn't shut up. I analysed the contours on my map. I looked at the woodblock ahead of me where the enemy was located. I regretted the multiple lumi pen points on my map, noting that the enemy was on a fold in the map and that I had folded it incorrectly. I called my section commanders in. Just before they arrived, I breathed slowly. I tried to silence my unsettled pinball machine and project composure. They took a knee.

'One Section, you're my assaulting section. Two Section, you're fire support. Three Section, you're my reserve. We're right-flanking through the stream and assaulting at ninety degrees through the woodblock.'

Each direction had to be given using the 'Brecon chop', a simple act that makes Army folk stand out like sore thumbs in the civilian world. You 'take a knee', one down, one up at right angles.

The arm extends out in the direction you wish to aim your troops towards, accompanied by a vertical open palm with fingers and thumb tightly together. Pointing is not permitted. Each gesture is held longer and more assertively than is comfortable.

'All okay?'

'Roger.'

'Roger.'

'Roger.'

And now we were ready to assault. As 2 Section continued to suppress the enemy, we withdrew back and sideways to a small and conveniently located hedgerow. There was another stream. Nobody wanted to go in. Colour Sergeant Campbell and Captain Connolly were lurking. I didn't have a choice. Into the drink I went and 1 Section grudgingly followed knowing that the rations in their trouser pockets were about to get soaked. We stayed low and moved through the water before hitting our 90-degree angle of assault. The job of the platoon commander isn't to close with and kill the enemy; that's the role of a section commander. I went firm, i.e. remained stationary. It was as if I now had to take my hand off the pinball controls and pass over to a specialist hoping they'd be as proficient as the one described by The Who in 'Pinball Wizard'.

According to Army doctrine, when assaulting an enemy position you move in bounds –sometimes known as 'leapfrogging'. It is the tactic of alternating movement to allow, if necessary, suppressive fire to enable forward movement. In this case, the assaulting eight-person section was split four and four between Charlie and Delta fireteams. As Charlie moved forward, Delta stayed stationary and, if necessary, provided fire support. When Charlie's bound was over, they went stationary to allow Delta to move and so on.

As they neared the enemy position, the four-person Charlie fireteam advanced with Delta providing cover. Concurrent to the discreet bounding, 2 Section continued to provide fire support from a 90-degree angle to distract the enemy, which allowed 1 Section to move forward stealthily to attack. On the radio, the assaulting section then ordered 2 Section to stop firing. Charlie was split into two and two as they bounded forward quickly and quietly. Finally, one pair remained to conduct the assault.

'Hard, fast and aggressive' was how Colour Sergeant Campbell said a final assault should be conducted.

At that stage, a grenade was thrown onto the enemy position and followed swiftly by the assaulting pair firing the necessary rounds to kill the enemy and take the position.

'REORG!'

As well as being the actual name of Captain Connolly's spaniel dog, 'reorg' signalled that the assault was complete, and all troops were to reassemble in the enemy position. 2 Section and 3 Section followed the route provided by 1 Section. They probably wished the stream wasn't there as their boots, socks and trousers got submerged in the unpleasantly bracing cold water.

The dead enemy were searched for additional weapons, maps and potentially useful information. The platoon then provided 360-degree protection, breathed heavily, looked out and awaited further orders.

'STOOOPPPPP! SAFETY CATCH! CLOSE IN!' Colour Sergeant Campbell's distinctive voice interrupted the silence. He was 100 metres away.

'TEN, NINE, EIGHT, SEVEN...' We ran over. 'Okay, gents, sit down, helmets off, notebooks out, pin your ears back.'

After each successful or failed attack, we would sit, fatigued, in a hollow square for a debrief, although depending on the time constraints and the situation, this could also just be a 'quick debrief' covering the essentials with the key people. I would be introduced to many more versions over the years including pre-briefs, post-briefs, down briefs, back briefs, point briefs, ground briefs, long briefs and brief briefs. Sometimes there were debriefs about down briefs and back briefs on ground briefs. With an enthusiastic Royal Gurkha Rifles officer named Captain Connolly as your platoon commander, there was even a level beyond the accepted 'hot debrief'. It was now possible to receive a 'piping hot debrief', its temperature clearly a factor in the timing of its delivery and potentially its content.

Without exception, his feedback was given from a little note-book on his webbing using the classic 'shit sandwich' technique: praise, followed by criticism (annoyingly rephrased as 'work-on' or 'learning' points) and then a touch of praise to end on a high. When he was done, Colour Sergeant Campbell would step up, likely reword a few of the points already made with an added sprinkling of shit for our already overloaded sandwich before stepping aside. Our opinions were meekly provided. Most people were more concerned with removing the damp and congealed contents of yesterday's ration pack from their pockets, hoping their map was sufficiently waterproofed and legible, squeezing the cold water out of their socks, wondering when and if they'd ever get dry and praying the next set of command appointments would allow them to kick the can of impending leadership responsibility down the road once more.

But then, as our endorphins kicked in and morale was reig-nited by the presence of talcum powder, fresh socks and an Army-issue fleece, it would happen again. Captain Connolly would stand alone on the empty side of the hollow square and face us. 'Gentlemen, command appointments...' And so would begin the next round of this merciless game. Issued kit was handed over, apologised for and signed for. The giver relieved, the receiver dismayed. And then off we went again in a new formation, across new ground and against a new enemy.

Brecon was unremitting and draining. Each stream was met with the command of 'Get right in and aboot it!' from Colour Sergeant Campbell. He was always testing us, always pushing our limits. Train hard, fight easy. Our basic skills and drills, use of the ground, delivery of orders and personal administration were commented upon and queried. There would be a series of 'Mr Stewart, just confirm'-type questions about all sorts of issues ranging from the presence of rust on the gas chamber of my rifle to the incorrect camouflage on my helmet. Others would get 'Just confirm' questions about their laces being undone, tactical over-sights or the use of white light in the harbour area. Some colour sergeants used a new array of phrases to provoke us into action. Things needed to be 'squared away'. 'Square away your bergen, Mr Mardirossoyan.' 'Square away your rubbish, Mr Russell.' 'Square away your life, Mr Cookson-Smyth.' It was their way of saying sort out/tidy/get a grip of whatever it was we needed to sort out/tidy/get a grip of.

Each evening, we'd watch Hexi TV as our Bean and Pasta Salad was heated to lukewarm temperature, to be eaten with the spoon that had accumulated dirt in our top pocket alongside a couple of lumi pens, a combi tool and compass. If Hexi TV didn't appeal, we'd clean our rifles which were likely damp, dirty and misfiring – much like those carrying them. If it was a special day, we'd treat ourselves to a two-course evening meal: perhaps a Potato and Leek Soup followed by a Pork Curry Nepalese Style. Once there were rumours of a three-course meal, but it was hard to nail three workable courses in one ration pack.

If the DS decided to 'bug us out' (i.e. force a withdrawal from our harbour area) with a surprise shot at an uncomfortable hour or time, such as midnight, mid-Hexi TV or rifle cleaning, officer cadets flailed, floundered and flapped. The occasional shot would go off, people would shout, 'CONTACT!' but be in too much of a frenzy to remember what to do. Or their rifle was still unassembled in 20 separate parts with baby wipes and brushes nearby so they couldn't do anything even if they wanted to. We went from thinking, 'Fuck off, I was asleep' to 'Fuck me, we're under contact' to 'Fuck it, let's put a plan together' to 'What a total fuck around...'

A once keen and thrusty cadet, Russell, had been in the UOTC and knew this game. He slept in his boots inside his bergen inside his sleeping bag inside his bivvy bag... just in case. Good drills, except for the lack of foot airing (which was bad drills). He slept with his rifle snug alongside him in his fart sack like a child with a teddy bear. Good drills, except for the frozen metal gradually ensuring he'd be hypothermic and sleep deprived come sunrise.

And so one time, bugged out at 0300, Russell immediately identifies the point of fire, yells, 'CONTACT FRONT!' and, Clear, Loud, As an order, with Pauses, gives a doctrinally impeccable target indication: 'TWO TIMES ENEMY. ONE O'CLOCK. FIFTY METRES. RAPID FIRE!' The one o'clock refers to the clockface method of bringing people's eyes to a target – three o'clock making people look right, six o'clock behind, nine o'clock left and so on. In his mind, this is Victoria Cross territory: leading, commanding, making decisions. The Sword of Honour beckons. While others flap, Russell changes magazines, yells, 'BACK IN!' and lays down fire support.

Cookson-Smyth, however, is distressed. Russell realises two rifles are better than one, so he supports the flailing Cookson-Smyth, whose boots are outside his sleeping bag along with his rusty rifle, and whose webbing is inside his bergen which has been rained on all night. Russell places his rifle on Cookson-Smyth's bergen. He successfully assists Cookson-Smyth but the enemy is bearing down fast. Russell then has what is known in Army terminology as 'an unthinking moment', which is to say a blank moment where panic overrides rationality. He and Cookson-Smyth run off together as others shout, 'WITHDRAW!' or the less heroic, 'RETREAT!' Upon reaching a safe area, it hits him. *Shit.*

It's horror: stomach-churning, intestine-whirring, head-spinning horror. He knows where it is, he can picture it, he can remember where and when he put it down. Maybe he can retrieve it before anyone notices, before the DS notice. Maybe they'll miss it when they move through the harbour area. The muzzle flashes from the advancing enemy make him turn around again. He tilts his head into his cupped hands. He continues the withdrawal with the rest of the platoon with both hands free but without the bit of metal that might protect him.

'STTTOOOOOPPPP!'

The shooting ceases and Colour Sergeant Campbell's distinctive voice overrides the sound of panting and cursing cadets.

'SAFETY CATCH! CLOSE IN!'

We form into a hollow square: 1 Section left, 2 Section middle and 3 Section right.

Campbell places the SA80 on the ground in front of his feet and steps back. People look around anxiously. In a calm voice, Campbell says, 'I think one of yous might be missing something. Sleep well, gents.' He turns and walks back into the darkness.

❧ — ❧

One more sleep – a few hours of gonk in our green hot dog sandwiched between two other folk – before we conducted the final assault and the end of the exercise (EndEx). To some, budding infanteers, we'd been living the dream. For others, dreams had been shattered by the reality of soldiering. Their visions of donning certain berets or following family traditions had evaporated with another failed command appointment, another jam sandwich biscuit (a ration pack Jammy Dodger) and another compromised recce patrol. The Regimental Selection Board (RSB) in Inters, the process through which your future cap badge and job role was determined, was competitive but also self-selective as people realised their heads and hearts were not aligned for certain potential job roles.

Before our sleep, we conducted what the padre called 'spiritual preparation for battle'. It wasn't exactly entering the Colosseum or charging at the gates of Mordor, but we did our best. There is a long-held connection between religion and the military. Historically, both sides, somewhat contradictorily, claimed to be conducting the will of God and declared that victory would justify the pain, heartache and suffering involved. Victory would prove that God was on their side. I'm not so sure what this meant for the souls of the defeated. Nowadays, the Sandhurst Haribo dispensers provide a sounding board and religious guidance without the uniform and rank slide. All padres, as well as dentists, doctors, lawyers and veterinarians, undergo their own four-week commissioning course at Sandhurst in order to qualify for their role. It's affectionately known as the 'Tarts and Vicars' course.

The sun was low in the sky and the members of CC133 were standing in a hollow square. It was the first time we had encountered Imjin Company all exercise. In the middle stood a padre, Father Cadogan, with a retro cassette player at his feet. We were each given an Order of Service. We said the Lord's Prayer, sang 'I Vow to Thee, My Country' and listened to the sermon.

Father Cadogan said that our performance in Brecon, however significant, was of less importance than having a wider understanding of our soldierly commitment. We should take pride in what we were doing and solace from the great men and women who had trodden similar paths before us. He read out the Oath of Allegiance we had each made in week one. On that occasion, with a new haircut, spanking new uniform and little clue about what was going on, or what was ahead, we had stood as intake in one of the most famous rooms of Old College, the Indian Army Memorial Room, and said the following words:

> *I do solemnly, sincerely and truly declare and affirm that I will be faithful and bear true allegiance to Her Majesty Queen Elizabeth II, her heirs and successors and that I will as in duty bound honestly and faithfully defend her Majesty, her heirs and successors in person, crown and dignity against all enemies and will observe and obey all orders of her Majesty, her heirs and successors and of the generals and officers set over me.*

It was one of the first times the wind had died and the rain had stopped. It was that golden hour when the deeper colours of the setting sun radiated across the Welsh hills. The padre's sermon concluded and we held a minute's silence. It was the first genuine moment of calm since stepping off the bus. It was a small opportunity to stop, think about those who had gone before, those who had supported us and those with whom we were standing shoulder to shoulder.

Father Cadogan's cassette machine then faltered under the pressure of its next command appointment, an obligatory rendition of 'Jerusalem'. It was, as always with members of the British Armed Forces – those who make that unambiguous commitment to their country – sincere and heartfelt. With the sun setting over the Brecon Beacons and several hundred voices singing, its poignancy was unmistakable.

In true Army fashion, once the sentimentality was over, it was back to reality. Colour Sergeant Campbell gathered us together. 'Gents, who the fuck took a Mr Whippy by the stag position?' It remains, even now, an unanswered question.

The morning's attack went without incident. The queen bees in command orchestrated, the rest scurried around executing orders. Without much notable defiance from the enemy – hat doffed once more to the ever-generous Gurkha Company Sittang – it was a rather one-sided affair, but the result satisfied the Sandhurst head honchos who had come to observe.

The real highlight, however, wasn't the first volley of fire support from 40 Platoon at H-hour (the moment we'd cross the line of departure), nor was it the final move from 41 Platoon to 'close with and kill the enemy'. The real highlight took place after both. It was the rallying cry of 'STOOOOPPPPPP!'

In this moment, EndEx is the best thing that could ever happen in life. The initial delirium is filled with gratitude: no more icy streams to crawl through or cold Chickpea Curry being tipped down your throat. You're also grateful you weren't spotted shooting an embarrassingly low firing rate, a key time saver in post-exercise rifle cleaning. Your elation is short-lived, however, curtailed by the call for a piping hot debrief or some angry Liverpudlian colour sergeant shouting, 'Start fucking cutting around!'

Our saviours, the 'white angels' – the same white buses that took us to Wales a week before – took us back to the Academy. Our 'horror bags' (packed lunches consisting of a white-bread sandwich, chocolate bar, pack of crisps, green apple and bottle of water) remained untouched as eyelids shut instantaneously and the sound of snoring filled the bus. As Sandhurst loomed, Colour Sergeant Campbell woke us and told us to put our berets on, as per dress regulations. These had not been worn once on exercise, not even for a second. We had last worn them prior to going to sleep on our journey to Wales. The light was fading as we placed our now-misshapen berets on our heads. We entered the gates, and clambered off the bus.

We re-entered our pristine rooms with hospital corners on our sheets, KFS sets on our shelves and Colour Sergeant Campbell's face on our mirrors saying, 'My Men, My Weapon, Myself. I am always in command appointment from the minute I wake.' I smiled wryly and thought about the priority alignment in South Wales for each person in 41 Platoon.

Having dumped our bergens, webbing, helmets and daysacks in our rooms, we faced a final personal admin dilemma knowing that we'd have a 0600 reveille. A shower was a given. Our hair was filthy and there was cam cream, oil, soot, dirt and other unidentified substances everywhere. The feeling post-wash – shampoo, conditioner, toothbrush, wet shave – was divine. The thought of platoon attacks, orders, magazine changes and firing positions vanished from our minds.

However, the good feeling evaporated in its turn when you re-entered your room. Your now-cleansed nostrils could smell the Welsh mud. Your damp and filthy boots sat haplessly in the middle of the floor. Your helmet was upturned, your webbing splayed out. Your bergen sat there like an unwanted guest grimly looking at back at you, an unwelcome reminder of where you'd been. In short, while you had returned to Sandhurst, your kit was still in Brecon and looked as if it was still on exercise.

This was where the dilemma lay. You had two options.

Either you could say, 'Fuck that, it can wait until tomorrow.' Excited, newly shaved and washed, you could set the alarm, peel back the sheets and clamber into bed knowing a well-warranted sleep awaited. Your unwanted guests would remain until tomorrow. Alternately you could say, 'Fuck it, let's get it done.' This meant unpacking, re-packing, checking, washing, soaking, drying, buffing, brushing, hoovering and polishing. You set alarms to tell you when the washing and drying cycles would end. You hung your bivvy bag and basher in the drying room, shook off the soil from your boots and bergen and aired your sleeping bags. You scrubbed your boots with hard-bristled brushes. You applied polish.

Either way, calls with girlfriends were delayed. You were still on exercise.

In Colour Sergeant Campbell's words, 'It isn't EndEx until you and your kit are ready to redeploy.'

⌒ — ⌒

On our CC133 wall calendar, we smugly crossed off a series of days having been out of camp. Each day in Wales was met with a big 'X'. The main challenge of the term was complete; our stint in Juniors was almost concluded. The final task would be attending the Senior term's Commissioning Parade before we 'popped smoke' for a week of Army Adventurous Training (AT) – caving, hill walking, Nordic skiing or orienteering – then home for Christmas leave. The AT was technically work, but it was not at Sandhurst, it was not in uniform, we could use each other's first names and there were no colour sergeants asking us to 'just confirm' our own actions.

Before that, we practised drill daily and tried to ignore the raft of irritable colour sergeants. If out of time, we were 'in clip'. In clip is a catch-all phrase covering a litany of errors. Helmet ajar and magazine pouches open: in clip. Languishing near the back of a group TAB panting heavily and sweating profusely: in clip. Being late for parade with the wrong equipment in the wrong order of dress: in clip.

If something went wrong, we were told to 'screw the nut' for Seniors. If you screw the nut in someone else's command appointment, you're giving your best performance. If you don't screw the nut, you're jacking on them and leaving them hanging out to dry in a command-appointment storm.

The days passed by and finally, accompanied by a beating drum, we and the Intermediate term cadets played a ceremonial supporting cast role on the parade square, standing behind the men and women of CC131 for their parade. They had completed the course. They had done all the exercises and ticked off all the days. The grandstand was full of proud parents, sisters, sons, daughters and friends, there to celebrate the commissioning of those future officers.

As I was holding the most uncomfortable drill position there is, presenting arms – standing rigidly with the butt of the five-kilogram rifle held out with the bayonet facing up – I saw a great friend slow-march his way towards the Old College steps. I was proud of him as a friend. It also reminded me of our end goal: earning a commission, becoming a British Army officer and joining our regiment. It was not our time, though, not yet. As they headed up those steps, we turned left and marched back to where we had come from.

'Has the situation changed?' our DS asked us to consider. Yes and no. In one day's time, we would still be officer cadets but a different kind to that of day one, week one: fitter, leaner, smarter, more efficient, more professional. So, having handed in our rifles, got out of our blues, packed our bags and changed into tweed jacket, shirt, tie and chinos, we turned our car keys to the right and left those gates for a much-appreciated break from Sandhurst.

Chapter 6

The two weeks of Christmas festivities, New Year's Eve embarrassments, catching up with girlfriends, boyfriends, friends and family that followed were a joy. It took a few days to rid the Army from my system, to accept a lie-in and conduct activities sequentially rather than concurrently. But that phase ended, thankfully replaced by family mocking, laughter, normality and relaxation. It was a relief to press an elongated pause and to think and process rather than to continually participate. Unfortunately, those two weeks had to end as the course schedule waited for nobody.

Dreading the return, Sunday night blues materialised. It was the kisses and long hugs from Sophie, my apologies, promises I'd call, hopes it would be different and reassurances we'd be okay. But driving back alone in the dark with a shirt and chinos on, a tweed jacket and tie on the passenger seat, made me begrudge my choices. I wanted to be in a T-shirt and tracksuit; to have soft pillows and a duvet, not a taut sheet and a blanket. The knowledge that the shout of 'On the Line!' would ring out within minutes of me opening my door, that a 0555 alarm loomed and that the joy of home was gone made me feel somewhat hollow.

To e-purge something on a Bowman radio is to give it a system reset – an unpopular and time-consuming action to perform. Humans, like Bowman radios, also have e-purge buttons. Time away from Sandhurst and people such as Colour Sergeant Campbell, Colour O'Sullivan, Captain Connolly and the CSM allowed us to click it wilfully. Returning was a shock to our systems.

'You couldn't fight your way out of a wet paper bag, Mr Stewart. GET A FUCKING MOVE ON!'

For reasons unbeknownst to us, our instructors for the post-leave 'shake out' exercise were switched. Colour Sergeant Campbell went to 40 Platoon and we had that impulsive Irishman, Colour O'Sullivan. He used terms such as 'brown taxis' for boots, 'tin hat' for helmet and 'eating irons' for cutlery. He was a man so deeply indoctrinated in the Army, I'm unreliably informed he made his family stand-to before their morning room inspection. He was as mockable as he was intimidating.

Macho concepts such as 'skin is waterproof' led, in his mind, in a logical progression to 'so don't wear Gore-Tex'. His justification was that 'It's better to be wet than dead.' This we all agreed on. Upon questioning whether being wet and being dead were mutually exclusive and whether it might be possible to be not wet and not dead, he simply said, 'If that was an invitation to speak, I would have sent it in the post.'

The Army's attitude to Gore-Tex was particularly contradictory and O'Sullivan exemplified this. Nothing ruffled O'Sullivan's prickly, camouflaged feathers quite like seeing a soldier in what was known as full 'crisp packet' – Gore-Tex jacket and trousers, which made a rustling sound more akin to a bespoke green-cheese-and-onion packet than discreet military uniform. Going full crisp packet was an accepted norm among very junior soldiers who naively believed that wearing full waterproof clothing in the rain was a wise strategy. Senior hard-nosed veterans also adopted this approach realising that clothing designed specifically for such conditions might serve an actual purpose.

For the other 95 per cent of soldiers, and for entirely unjustifiable reasons, wearing Gore-Tex was neither seen as practical nor 'ally'. And without those two boxes ticked, it was hard to persuade them to wear it. Quite why not wearing appropriate clothing was better than wearing it made no sense then and it makes no sense now. 'Ally' was an almost indescribable combination of stylish and anti-regulation which might sound antithetical to notions of standardisation and conformity. It was a slight teenage-rebel phase meeting a midlife crisis but in a military context.

O'Sullivan was a strong proponent of 'free phys' when applied to casualty evacuations and leopard-crawling. He simplified instructing at Sandhurst to 'Your job as junior officers is fucking simple: deliver orders and don't get lost.' On one extraction, Norton lost a magazine during a change. He panicked and chose not to return and collect it. O'Sullivan swooped.

'A FUCKING MAGAZINE! IS THIS COURSE A JOKE TO YOU, MR NORTON?' With a lowered voice but still seething, he continued, 'A magazine is thirty rounds. Thirty rounds is thirty dead enemy. Thirty dead enemy is thirty people who won't shoot you and thirty people who won't shoot you is thirty coffins that won't have to be explained to your parents.'

Not everyone had spent Christmas in the UK. Naj Abil, 41 Platoon's Afghan foreign cadet, had flown back home during his free fortnight. Ten days of that was spent on patrol with assault rifle and pistols serving in the Afghan Army. We were devouring our body weight with roast potatoes and mince pies as he engaged Al Qaeda at close range in the dusty streets of his hometown. It's hard to know what to say to someone when they've flown 5,000 miles from a genuine life-and-death situation to being told to dry their sink with a towel because a broken tap dripped on it. When they've gone from shooting at humans shooting back at you and seeing friends blown up, to being told how to load a magazine and safely handle your assault rifle in a classroom. But to his immense credit, he just smiled, stayed composed and got on with it. In its own way, it was a lesson to us all.

Part of the dread of Sandbags was the initial shock, the shake-out exercise, orders, marching, room inspections, fitness tests and show parades – but also Exercise FIRST ENCOUNTER. This was the Bogeyman lurking in the shadows, the exercise all officers spun dits, or ditties, about – stories that, like fishermen's yarns, were invariably exaggerated for effect. FIRST ENCOUNTER was the first major exercise in Inters and it came around quickly. We barely had time to march correctly again before being launched into chemical, biological, radiological and nuclear training and the basics of defensive military tactics, which provided an unfortunate combination of ingredients. The only time we'd had the pleasure of wearing CBRN outfits thus far was that deeply disturbing, eye-watering Tabasco dose of CS gas we were subjected to in Juniors. Still, it wasn't worth over-thinking for now. One day at a time.

In British football, when people discuss the best players, an age-old question can be posed: 'Can they do it on a cold, wet, windy day in February?' FIRST ENCOUNTER, a winter defensive CBRN exercise, is the Sandhurst equivalent. This is when the basics are of less importance than your ability to endure, your resilience. As the saying goes, 'When the going gets tough, the tough get going.' Or, as I learned from a former climbing partner, 'Human beings are like tea bags. You only know how strong they are when you put them in hot water.'

Before we got to the gas masks and trenches, however, we had migrated from Old College to New College and from Juniors to Inters. New College was a larger building – the famous red-brick one with ill-advised green panelling lining the interior corridors. With the move came several exciting changes. First, and most important, we were no longer at the bottom of the food chain.

Beneath us were Junior term cadets tick-tocking in their coveralls and getting their hair cut (although Colour Sergeant Campbell lost no time in reminding us that we'd soon be joining them if we didn't improve). Second, we had new rooms – okay, more different than exciting. Third, we didn't have a morning water parade or national anthem singing. Fourth, we had the New College dining room. It was still a big room, adorned with military paintings and long wooden tables, but mealtimes were *slightly* less rushed, the food was *slightly* better and, most excitingly, there were pains au chocolat for breakfast. In the grand scheme of things, a few French pastries alongside Army-issue coffee, a bowl of muesli and a poached egg was hardly deal-breaking stuff; that buttery chocolatey goodness was not going to make the PT sessions any easier or CBRN training any less unpleasant. But those small things made the daily grind slightly more bearable and, as such, felt like progress.

⌒ – ⌒

The members of CC133 hurried up and waited, loading bergens and collecting rifles, handing out horror bags and meeting five minutes before the five minutes before deadline. Finally, though, we made it to Thetford, Norfolk, for Exercise FIRST ENCOUNTER.

What lay ahead sounded unpleasant. Your team of four built a trench of exact dimensions: the height of the tallest person, the width of a shovel and a length of four metres. You de-turfed the ground, placed it to one side and dug down. As The Kinks would say, 'All day and all of the night', although their version was rather more enticing than ours. You kept going until the whole platoon, and indeed the whole company, was 'dug in', i.e. sufficiently prepared to defend against an attack. Wouldn't a JCB be quicker and less labour-intensive than hacking at the frozen Norfolk ground in February? Yes, it would, immeasurably, indescribably easier. But that was not very Sandhurst and wouldn't teach us the fundamentals of what might be required. So we dug hour after hour while those wishful JCB thoughts drifted through our minds.

Concurrently, our CBRN 'state of readiness' was heightened incrementally as our fears of the call of 'GAS! GAS! GAS!' increased. To begin the exercise, the DS notified us of the minimal threat so we dug equipped with a rifle, helmet and gas mask a few metres away. It was just us and our entrenching tools. To civvies, this might be a fold-up shovel but, in the Army, and in Thetford, it was known as an entrenching tool. The DS increased the CBRN threat at irregular intervals through Orders Groups (O-Groups), via the temporary platoon commander, and we reacted by bringing our gas masks and rifles closer while gradually adding CBRN clothing as we continued digging. Each phase and layer added inconvenience and discomfort.

The culmination of our readiness states was 'Four Romeo', a state of maximum discomfort and minimal spatial awareness. This was full Chernobyl. You were in combat fighting order with your ammunition and equipment belt, rifle and helmet as well as your CBRN equipment. The latter consisted of an ill-fitting coverall made of hazard-protective material; cotton inner gloves and outer gloves more akin to Shrek-sized Marigolds; outer boots like large wellies; a satchel containing needles, powder and spare canisters; a hood; and, best of all, a gas mask. Whatever happened to you in life, however tired and uncomfortable you were, it could always be made worse by wearing Four Romeo. We continued digging.

Our situation could only have become worse if an Irish instructor had wandered over at 0200 and told us to 'start cutting around' because, if we didn't, he'd turn us into a 'puddle of piss'. Inside our suits, regardless of the face we put on, each of us was probably slowly melting into a piss puddle anyway. We dreaded the inevitability of it all. And depressingly, the result was inevitable – a drawn-out episode of emotional, physical and psychological hardship over which we had no control.

Sleep deprivation is a great leveller. Lots of people are effective when they're well-rested, well-prepared, clean, sated and chirpy. That's not what Sandhurst tests you for, though. It wants you to perform at your best when you're at your worst, not when you're at your best.

After a long night, I was on a ten-minute break with Philipps while the other two dug. This was how we got through the nights, ten minutes being long enough to rest the body and mind but short enough not to get a chill from frozen sweat. My eyes were open but my brain was blank, grateful not to be digging but dreading starting again. Philipps and I passed my flask of Army-issue cofftea between us in silence. Cofftea was a peculiar and uniquely Army-tasting beverage indistinguishably combining two of the world's favourite hot drinks. It was rarely loved, requested or praised, but it was appreciated in situations such as this.

I looked out, readjusted my eyes to the darkness and looked again. I could see them coming. My mind was alert, certain of what I was seeing and concerned about how events would unravel. The enemy was descending from the hills beyond. They were moving from tree to tree, scurrying and leopard-crawling, quietly but en masse. This was the imminent attack we'd been waiting for. It was time to act and it had to be quick; we had to gain momentum, take the initiative. Everyone needed to be informed so we could defend our ground or coordinate a counterattack. With every second of indecision, the enemy moved closer, wave after wave. I knew what I had to do but just sat and watched, captivated by their deliberate movements and too fearful to say anything to anyone else. I finally leant over to Philipps who was sitting next to me, blank-faced and seemingly uninterested in the enemy's approach.

'Mate, what should we do?' I whispered.

'About what?'

'The Gurkhas. Look at them. We need to tell someone.'

'Huh? There's nothing out there. Are you alright, mate?'

'Yeah, yeah, fine. You? Just planning for all eventualities.'

I continued to look around anxiously. I blinked, rubbed my eyes and looked again, but said nothing more. A few hours later, the sun rose and I looked out again. All I could see were grass and trees, the same grass and trees I had been looking at all night. The same grass and trees I had been convinced were swarming hordes of enemy forces. I was grateful I hadn't said anything more. All over the place, officer cadets were asleep on their feet – and elsewhere, as a member of 41 Platoon went to a Portaloo for a number two only to be heard snoring by Colour O'Sullivan shortly afterwards. Having identified the culprit, Norton, O'Sullivan promptly informed him that it was 'hideous drills' and he should stand by for a 'melting' back at camp. An uneasy few days lay ahead for him.

O'Sullivan clocked a theme and stood on watch for repeat offenders for the next few days. A few evenings later, the unfortunate cadet happened to be Cookson-Smyth. O'Sullivan, who had been lying in wait, sensed his moment. He crept forward and put his ear to the plastic. As anticipated, the sound of contented snoozing was heard from within. Rather than launching into a Q and A, O'Sullivan had a different plan. O'Sullivan opened a canister of CS gas, pulled slightly on the top of the door, squeezed the canister inside and uttered those three unlovable words, 'GAS! GAS! GAS!'

Being gassed, even at the best of times – if there is such a thing – is awful, let alone when you've resorted to slinking off into a mobile plastic toilet cubicle for a few minutes of shuteye. It somehow combines the internal claustrophobia of being forced to hold your breath underwater with the discomfort of being used as target practice at a pepper-spraying contest.

Rushed noises coming from within the receptacle were the first sign of Cookson-Smyth's alarm. The lock indicator then switched from red to green, occupied to vacant, and a dazed, confused and spluttering officer cadet came stumbling out.

'An embarrassment, Mr Cookson-Smyth' was all O'Sullivan said before heading back into the darkness.

In the days that followed, the stories and errors were as plentiful as they were absurd. Shahid from Abu Dhabi politely declined the opportunity to take his turn at sentry duty. 'No, Colour Sergeant, I won't be going on stag,' he said to Campbell before feebly grasping his entrenching tool and motioning towards the hole in front of him. This refusal did not go down well, though, and Shahid was warned he would be fined a month's wages if he refused to comply.

'Colour Sergeant, how much is a month's wages?'

'About two thousand English pounds, Mr Shahid.'

'Colour Sergeant, I will happily pay two thousand pounds every month if it means I do not have to go on stag again.' As responses go, it was commendable.

On sentry duty on night three of the exercise, two members of 41 Platoon are the first line of defence for the hundreds of soldiers still digging behind them. Their job is to be alert, awake and prepared for all eventualities. Sentries are posted on one-hour rosters in pairs at night. They have warning signals, several means of communication and plenty of silent thinking time. Mostly, though, they're looking at nothing and nothing happens, which suits all involved. As their changeover time dawns, they look again at their watches wondering at how time is moving so slowly. Finally, their replacements arrive to relieve them.

They mutter the odd word to each other in the handover process – arcs of fire, means of communications, notable features – before they get up to move. Knowing a return from stag means going back to a hole in the ground and an entrenching tool, however, the thought is a touch unappetising. They stop. Perhaps being on stag is a blessing. So, the four of them sit and talk in muffled voices through their gas masks.

The acting platoon commander, Goff, a thrusting top-third cadet with a laser-beam focus on a competitive regiment, notices a break in communications between the trenches and moves to the stag position to check on his men. Excellent leadership. After an initial enquiry, the five of them conclude it isn't so bad. They sit together but the conversation slows as the silence and darkness dominate their senses. In each of them, exhaustion sets in. Their eyelids gain weight by the minute. Each blink is extended by a second. They know falling asleep isn't permissible. One by one, though, their input to the conversation comes to a halt. One by one, their resolve yields as their eyes close within the worlds of their own gas masks. All five 41 Platoon heroes lie face down on the floor, gas masks on, rifles by their sides and dead to the world around them.

Gunfire breaks the silence. Automatic weapons. It's *very* close.

'CONTACT!' Goff's reaction is instinctive.

The firing is painfully close. In fact, it's coming from right behind them. Just as instinctively, all five of them reach for their rifles to engage the enemy. They turn around.

Colour Sergeant Campbell stands in front of them with an SA80 in each hand, his fingers hovering over the triggers. Three more rifles are slung around his shoulders. He stops firing.

'Morning, gents.'

There are no words, no excuses and no comebacks.

In a normal military context, sleeping on stag is a court-martial offence. FIRST ENCOUNTER, however, is an exercise designed to push you to your limits and beyond. A version of this CBRN defensive exercise has occurred at Sandhurst for decades and will likely continue. In 41 Platoon alone, we hid cadets under stacks of bergens so they could sleep for a few hours without getting caught by the DS as they became too 'combat ineffective' for their own good. People wandered into the woods, got lost and slept in stinging nettles; others slept standing up in their trenches. People's supplies of Pro Plus ran out and uncontrollable shaking fits led them to the medical tent. Others misjudged the combined effect of Red Bull, cofftea, sleep deprivation, gas masks and ration packs, leading to a situation where they were uncontrollably active at both ends. People's tactical awareness and decision-making ability went out the window. My moving-trees scenario was scratching at the surface of ignominy.

One legendary story was told about a colour sergeant who, a few years earlier, had apparently ridden a mountain bike in the wee hours across the training area wearing a pink-elephant costume. He was not stopped and nobody said a word. It was an example of the kind of state of delusion it was anticipated that we would each at some stage be in. The story is so ridiculous, it might just be true.

Every commissioned officer has their own FIRST ENCOUNTER dits to spin about hallucinations, hiding cadets, hoarding non-issue rations, sleeping on stag and refusing orders. FIRST ENCOUNTER was five days of bitter cold, digging and getting gassed. Given that simple description, it begs the question of why anyone would ever, could ever, volunteer for the experience. And yet, that's why the Bear said, 'If it was easy, everyone would do it.' Fundamentally, it isn't easy and so not everyone does it. More than the digging and the gassing, what the exercise provided was more shared experiences, shared hardship and the breaking down of more mental and physical barriers. It showed us what could be achieved individually and collectively and thus was another example of what Sandhurst was all about.

━━━

Our platoon had lost three people in Junior term from injuries, loss of motivation and failing the Service Test. If Juniors was part of the breaking phase of Sandhurst, where people's focus was questioned and their willingness to endure and show resilience were put to the test, it worked. Post-FIRST ENCOUNTER, 41 Platoon welcomed in five new officer cadets – D'Agnolio, Daniels, Ismay, Reynolds and Sarwani from Afghanistan – to take our number from 27 to 32. For different reasons, all five had been held back in Lucknow Platoon but would now aim to finish the course alongside us.

The Sovereign's Banner Competition is an inter-platoon competition at Sandhurst with the banner awarded to the highest-performing platoon in the intake. Scores are based on continual assessments throughout the course in everything from navigation and drill to fitness and academic achievement. The platoon the five newbies were joining was tightknit, high-spirited and professional but consistently underperforming in the Sovereign's Banner. Collectively we viewed the contest with indifference as it seemed the wrong sort of game-playing; our priorities of cohesion, togetherness and competence in the field were both less tangible and less popular with the DS. As such, not even halfway through the term, we were mathematically out of the race, now just in a tense battle for the wooden spoon with 37 Platoon from Imjin Company.

Now, though, we could continue the 'build' phase of officer training away from digging trenches. The basic soldiering element, which had given a head start on Ironing Board Sunday to ex-UOTC graduates, Army cadets and ex-rankers, had now been somewhat reeled in and there was a more level playing field as we began a new phase. As much as we needed to know how to close with and kill the enemy by posting grenades, or march with our mouths shut and arms shoulder-high, our role as officers was primarily to lead, manage, organise, motivate and empower those under our command when we commissioned. This is what Sandhurst now had to build in us. Unconsciously following orders, as we did in Juniors, was important, essential in fact, but now we needed to think independently. As such, we had to temporarily put aside the cam cream, ammunition and target indications and try to spark life into the grey matter in our heads. This was part of the 'Faraday Five' period – five weeks where more time was spent in the classroom with Captain Connolly in the academic wing, Faraday Hall, than in the field.

The Combat Estimate, or the 'Seven Questions', is the British Army's operational planning tool. It encourages rational thinking through a methodical process of questioning aiming to reduce bias and enable leaders to rationally make the best decisions. The Seven Questions are:

1. What is the situation and how does it affect me?
2. What have I been told to do and why?
3. What effects do I need to achieve and what direction must I give to develop my plan?
4. Where can I best accomplish each action/effect?
5. What resources do I need to accomplish each action/effect?
6. When and where do the actions take place in relation to each other?
7. What control measures do I need to impose?

We learned the Combat Estimate to structure our thoughts. We were constantly bombarded with clichéd mantras such as 'Failure to plan is planning to fail' and 'Planning is essential but plans are useless', as well as with a version of the Seven Ps: 'Proper Planning and Preparation Prevents Piss Poor Performance.' The Combat Estimate taught us that our instincts were not always right and to trust the process. We used this at the tactical level; the brigadiers and generals used the same structure strategically. This was Officer Education 101, our bread and butter. In practice, some took to it like ducks to water, others like Bambi on ice with their brains overthinking, underthinking and scrambling with each additional question.

The final Combat Estimate test was known as 'PRACTAC'. In this, we had to stand in front of commissioned officers, having analysed the ground in front of us as well as our strengths, weaknesses, dispositions, intentions and equipment, and those of the enemy. We had to explain our role within the intent of our commanders, key considerations and the impact of nearby forces, and finally choose from one of our three courses of action (COAs). We had to brief this using a model built from sticks, labels, small cardboard ammunition boxes representing buildings, pebbles representing roads and moss representing fields. We were graded simply as Fail, Satisfactory or Good.

Nobody in CC133 wanted to be the one late to parade, in the wrong uniform or holding up the platoon. They also, however, didn't crave the punchy, pressurised command appointments or excessive responsibility. They thought they did but they didn't *really*. They sought a 'Good' in PRACTAC but were satisfied with a 'Satisfactory' as it wasn't a 'Fail'. The Army needs most soldiers to be in this category. The odd free-thinking maverick is beneficial but not everyone can willingly select which orders and rules they choose to follow. In short, not everyone can be an Admiral Nelson.

Regular performance reviews, including of SMART (Specific, Measurable, Achievable, Realistic and Timely) goals, were part of the dual Sandhurst focus on competitiveness and self-improvement. Each platoon and company was different, but the intake and generational patterns had remained consistent for decades. The time we'd spent together, almost half a year, had been intense, far exceeding that with our families. We slept next to those in our platoon more often than with our girlfriends. Each misdemeanour, show parade or command-appointment calamity was visible. We knew those we served with. Not everything about their lives – it took months to accumulate people's first names, let alone their backgrounds – but everything about their conduct within the platoon.

Someone compared Sandhurst and the platoon to Willy Wonka's Chocolate Factory. There were some obvious flaws to this comparison, there being no golden-ticket selection policy, chocolate rivers, glass elevators or Oompa-Loompas, to name a few. However, the image of us as little workers churning away inside a bigger machine was true.

We had names on our chests but even they became impersonal. Captain Connolly clamped down on this pronto when someone once referred to me as Geordie. 'Gents, who the fuck is Geordie? Let's cut this Geordie crap. It's Mr Stewart.'

We were our Army numbers and surnames; we had become Mr Men. And that was also why the Willy Wonka analogy, just as the Harry Potter one, sort of worked. Nobody from the outside really understood what happened. Nobody in other intakes, other companies, other platoons really understood *your* platoon. Despite the impersonality Sandhurst tried to impose, an unavoidable familiarity and bond was created with those you were alongside, perhaps because of what the system was trying to impose. We recognised the way people walked, marched and ran; the way they spoke, coughed and cleared their throats. We knew when our neighbours went to bed and woke up by various sounds: plugs entering sockets, alarms going off or, in the case of Mr Sarwani to my left, the recitation of morning prayers.

As people's flaws and failings came to the surface (and surface they did, often very visibly) the platoon dynamics shifted. Some said it was part of the natural filtering process. There was also a harshness, occasionally a dismissiveness, directed towards those who wouldn't, or couldn't, perform at the necessary level. The 'If you can't take the heat, get out of the kitchen' idea was sometimes part of Sandhurst's functioning. When the heat increased beyond bearable levels, there was no way out of the kitchen except with an ironing board under your arm. So most people just got on with it. You made a mistake and were severely mocked for it; then life continued. A few days later, someone else would make a mistake and receive the same harsh treatment. You learned and didn't repeat the mistake. It was part of the journey. Given the closeness of the platoon and the overarching knowledge that you *had* to work together, that you were only as strong as your weakest part, the ethos was to build people up rather than vindictively knock them down.

Nicknames were part of platoon-bonding. Rarely did anyone choose their nickname. Rather, it was awarded to you and, as such, lay beyond your control. Nicknames and the Army had always gone (and would continue to go) hand in hand. It was group bonding. In this respect, Sandhurst was no different to team situations the world over.

Following his miserable experience in the CBRN chamber, Yarrow's nickname of Casper stuck. Patel was known as 'Smurfette' after an unfortunate incident involving an upturned Portaloo, while Fyfe was awarded 'Victorian Grandad' for behaviour more appropriate to the late 19th century. Kieliszewski was called 'Letters' after a PTI failed to pronounce his name properly. ('Mr Keelezki, Queueovski, Quilloosky... whatever it is... oi... "Letters", get over here.') Reagan became 'Hodor' for drawing unfavourable comparisons with the Game of Thrones character, just as Norton did with 'Ephialtes' from *300*. Travers became 'Punchy' after reacting pugnaciously to some verbal jibing. Lloyd became 'Dumbo' for possessing, in his own words, 'a distinguished Roman nose'. 'Big Gay Al' Hammond was neither big nor gay, nor called Al, but the name stuck. Goff, about the most competitive man in NATO in everything from queuing to dating, was given 'Elevenerife' for the simple reason that, if you had been to Tenerife, he had most certainly been to Elevenerife. Bondelevitch was 'Civvy' because, despite six months of intensive military training, he remained a civilian in combats. Simpson was called 'Cat Killer Simmo' for reasons it probably isn't best to delve into. Agnew, aka 'Barry', bore a striking resemblance to one of the Chuckle Brothers. Lockwood had to accept 'Eeyore' for displaying a permanently overcast mood. Lombard had one hand smaller than the other so was called the 'Clock'.

The real 41 Platoon nickname hero was Officer Cadet Francis, also known as the 'Commodore'. The nickname emerged from (entirely justified) accusations of jack behaviour including a few dodgy stag rosters and selectively ignored WhatsApp messages. A natural extension was calling him 'Captain Jack', after Captain Jack Sparrow of *Pirates of the Caribbean*. Several people were known as jack but this guy was the jackest of them all. Captain wasn't sufficient. Sticking with the naval theme, we needed a suitably high rank to represent his approach. The 'Commodore' he thus became.

With his cover blown, the Commodore's initial Sandhurst philosophy of 'It's about being jack without appearing to be jack' had to change. It subsequently became 'It's about being jack while appearing to be jack.' A double, perhaps even a triple, agent. Hidden in plain sight. The anti-officer. Brazenly unhelpful and shamelessly set on achieving every task with the minimum expenditure of effort, the Commodore was as passionate about delegation as he was content in the middle of the bottom-third; unwilling and unable to go up but safe in the knowledge that a few hopeless souls would regularly reside beneath him.

As with legal tax avoidance, you needed to understand the system to beat the system. The Commodore understood Sandhurst. He knew what did and didn't need to be done to earn a commission. As such, he masterfully played according to his rules, and the rules to earn a commission. Being aware of being jack is one thing, being unaware and being jack is another. The former is far less dangerous than the latter. There was something almost admirable about the Commodore's approach. He was a master at the game and yet didn't play it. Unlike so many who put on a face, he never shied away from being himself.

Chapter 7

The original classrooms and dormitory of Sandhurst, now named Old College, were completed in 1812. It is an imposing two-storey building, displaying a broad, pale cream façade, with the main parade ground to its southeast and the Grand Entrance supported by eight stone columns. Sitting atop the building are two statues: one of Mars, the Roman god of war, the other of Minerva, the Roman goddess of wisdom. As a combination, they represent the fundamental aims of Sandhurst. As an officer, you need the tactical skills and leadership to perform in battle combined with the empathy, intelligence and pragmatism to understand your soldiers. Sandhurst continually tries to instil these values, and that of its motto, 'Serve to Lead'.

Mars and Minerva are symbolic of the structure of the commissioning course. You bounce from PT to the ranges to the communications wing to the lecture theatre to academic classrooms. You can go from charging around with a 100-kilogram log on your shoulders to firing assault rifles from 400 metres to learning about Clausewitz, Cialdini and Churchill. You need to understand the history of warfare and modern behavioural scientific theory as much as you need to be able to deliver quick battle orders under pressure and perform lifesaving first aid.

Mars and Minerva, body and mind, were constantly being tested and tweaked. We were told to ignore the breaking-and-rebuilding rumour; we were selected for our potential for leadership, not expected to be leaders already. There were then contradictions as we were thrust into command appointments and assessed on our ability to sink or swim. Sandhurst constantly created situations to provoke us, either positively or negatively. Often Sandhurst was a series of small individual or collective tests, specifically designed to generate a particular reaction.

Learning to soldier – Mars training – is an essential part of the Army. Everyone, male or female, recce soldier or medic, electrical engineer or signaller, needs a basic soldiering level. This is for your individual capability while developing a broader understanding of what those at the sharp end do. An infantry officer who gave us a talk on his deployment to the Falkland Islands said, 'The infantry is the final six feet of British foreign policy.' Aspiring infanteers went weak at the knees as they salivated at the prospect of sunrise bayonet charges. The Army has multiple purposes but the basic principle of taking another human life is something you need to come to terms with, regardless of what part of the Army you join.

DRUID'S RIDGE was the second key exercise of Inters. It was not the final test of the term, as our regimental careers would be decided only a few weeks later at RSBs, but it was an opportunity to impress the DS at the midway point of the course. These were the final games of the season before the big cup final, an opportunity to put yourself in the manager's mind for the team selection.

The night before, we laminated, deliberated over sock numbers, packed and re-packed our bergens and finally turned off the lights in the wee hours. The morning was filled with the usual dramas: an unnecessarily early coach-loading time, an acerbic lance corporal armourer giving us weapons, an unsatisfying early breakfast, a final mini-flap about overlooked items, a final visit to an actual loo and the provision of an Army-issue horror bag for the drive. Hurry up and wait. We slept along the M4, over the bridge into Wales, along the winding roads until that sharp right turn took us over a small bridge, over a cattle grid, and into the Brecon Beacons.

It was approaching April. Much of the UK was joyfully saying 'Spring has sprung' as lambs were bouncing, birds were migrating and clocks were soon shifting forwards. Winter was over. Brecon, however, was selectively ignorant of occurrences elsewhere and content with its own microclimate. Weather-wise, Brecon is the British Army's trump card. Four seasons in a day, unpredictable and unwisely underestimated. We, the questionably valiant and resilient members of 41 Platoon, would have to cope with whatever it threw at us. 'God's country', people called it. We decided that God must have a fine and enviable supply of Gore-Tex, warm-weather clothing, hot brews and morale.

This exercise was more complicated than those before it. We were introduced to Fighting in Built-Up Areas (FIBUA) – basically fighting with buildings and people around you rather than woodblocks. This required many more considerations and permutations than a rural setting. FIBUA was also affectionately referred to as 'FISCH', which stood for 'Fighting In Some Other Cunt's House'. Barbed-wire defences and minefields were constructed whilst the houses were boarded up to minimise likely entry points. This was part of the defensive element of the exercise to focus our minds on security, preventative measures and threat assessments. Alongside this, there was the consistent battle rhythm of recce patrols and disruptive actions including raids and ambushes. It also included the CBRN elements of FIRST ENCOUNTER, thankfully without the digging.

The tempo was akin to that of CRYCHAN'S but with multiple threats, more complex scenarios and elongated command appointments. We had greater flexibility and responsibility, greater room for manoeuvring and mistake-making. For those in command, emphasis was placed on balancing risk versus reward, tactics versus strategy, and assessing potential collateral damage – all critical elements of decision-making that also shone a brutal light on wayward judgement and poor performance under pressure.

Captain Connolly continued to play command appointment games as 41 Platoon persisted in shying away from assignments. But we all had that fear, instilled by the looming RSBs, that we had to do something to prove our worth. Captain Connolly reliably utilised the famous Army Pose-Pause-Pounce method of asking questions.

'Right, gentlemen, what are the principles of FIBUA?'

We were sitting in a hollow square taking sips from our water bottles and clutching the remnants of our ration packs, which had become disappointingly malformed in the previous platoon attack. Having posed the question, Connolly paused in wait. Nobody wanted to answer incorrectly; it was far wiser to play it safe. Connolly's gaze flickered around the group, the whites of his eyes standing out clearly against the green-and-black cam cream. Waiting for weakness, he saw it everywhere: the sheepish looks to either side, the downward glances, the nervous swigs of water, the faux notetaking, the confident double bluffing – everyone had a tell. And then came the pounce, the moment of truth, in which it was determined whether you, an unknowing cadet, would get away with it or whether your doctrinal ignorance would dimly shine through.

'Misterrrr...' The pounce hung suspended in mid-air, like a super slow-motion sequence from *Planet Earth*. The bullet was coming for someone, but we didn't know whom. Maybe Connolly didn't know either. But still it went on. 'Rrrrr...' Nobody made eye contact at this point. 'Russell.' The bullet hit its mark.

Poor Russell had no idea of the principles of FIBUA, but he did his best to answer. When Connolly realised he was flogging a dead horse, he swung around seeking another victim. 'Help him out, Misterrrr... Stewart.' And so the games continued.

The exercise itself was conducted in what the Army called 'inclement conditions on undulating terrain'. In normal parlance, this meant cold, wet and windy. We were fatigued, exasperated and perplexed. It was soldiering in Brecon. What else would you expect?

We played more games of Hexi TV as our vacant minds found solace in the gradual heating of the silver packets of chemically engineered food, the neutered flame struggling hard to keep us, and itself, at a workable operating temperature. When feeling particularly demoralised, we compounded our self-loathing by spooning in portions of cold ration-pack meals, not trusting the time allocated to us by the DS.

At regular intervals before and during this exercise, Captain Connolly questioned us about our performance 'at this stage of the commissioning course'. Oddly, whatever stage we were at, we always seemed to be behind where he thought we should be. Maybe it gave us something to work towards. Cookson-Smyth and Mardirossoyan were informed that they couldn't organise 50-per-cent leave in a two-man submarine as they unsuccessfully tried to dig a shell scrape and conduct personal administration at the same time. Meanwhile Colour Sergeant Campbell continually reminded us to 'Get yas notebooks out and pin yas ears back' whenever any brief – down brief, back brief, ground brief or debrief – was taking place. The Commodore had an unfortunate personal incident during a night recce patrol where he slightly lost control of his bowels and had to be removed by the 'jack wagon', the first-aid Land Rover which was, as usual, driven by an unsympathetic private soldier. We huddled under bashers and cleaned our rifles in hollow squares. At one tragic stage, the exercising troops of CC133, upon running out of ammunition, were informed that we had to shout 'Bang!' instead of firing anything.

We were increasingly confused by military terminology as we learned about Forward Line of Own Troops (FLOT) and Forward Line of Enemy Troops (FLET) before understanding our own Surveillance Target Acquisition Plan (STAP). This would often get called a STAP Plan which, for the beady-eyed amongst you, is essentially saying Surveillance Target Acquisition Plan Plan. With the number of acronyms thrown around, often by well-meaning but ignorant folk, such repetitions were not uncommon. We were obsessed by our Area of Operations (AO) and the locations of nearby Friendly Forces (FF), just as we scrutinised Named Areas of Interest (NAI) without ever actually naming them.

We concluded that, given the Army's total aversion to writing the time 0000, and instead opting for 2359 or 0001, the stroke of midnight would be an effective time to launch an attack. We made odd statements about trees and bushes providing cover from view and fire or cover from view but not cover from fire. We were given hard-to-comprehend and slightly contradictory statements such as 'Slow is smooth and smooth is slow' whilst also being ordered to 'cut about'.

We discussed the true dream of all of us on exercise: boots-off gonkers. Not just normal gonking, but next level gonking, where you could unroll your green hot dog, remove your trousers, maybe even your pants if you were so inclined, and finally, crucially, take off your boots. But boots-off gonkers wasn't really a thing; it was more of a mirage, an unachievable, inaccessible fantasy, a utopia that lay forever beyond our clutching grasp. Boots-off gonkers was also that one thing we all clung onto at different points: it was hope. We knew that it would never, could never, materialise; but that was the point. It didn't stop us dreaming.

As with the CBRN phase on FIRST ENCOUNTER, suitable amounts of disruptive chaos were thrown into the mixer by the DS. Colour Sergeant Campbell, who assigned each of the three 41 Platoon sections to three separate empty buildings. We were given time to fortify them with appropriate defences, including broken furniture and sandbags. We were also gifted with the immortal words, 'Gents, you're in your own time now.' This is usually a good thing, a chance to finally relax away from prying DS eyes. On exercise, though, we existed in a state of permanent distrust, almost of fear, of the DS. Accordingly, we were unwilling to wait, relax or sleep when told to do so. We were wary of the allocated timings for cooking and sleeping. 'Once bitten, twice shy', as they say. We had all been bitten and caught with our pants down – literally and metaphorically – when we weren't prepared. 'Never again' we told ourselves.

Hammond was lying half-asleep with his section in building 12. He had thought about, but wisely opted against, boots-off gonkers. Instead, he did what we all did, which was to adopt a state of unrelaxed relaxation, attentive idleness, that default setting when you're told you're in your own time. In a matter of seconds, the situation changed dramatically. Colour sergeants Campbell and O'Sullivan stormed the building with gas masks on, threw CS canisters around and shouted, 'GAS! GAS! GAS!' Pandemonium ensued. Everyone covered their faces and reached for their gas masks. Once the masks were deployed, pulse rates dropped and rationality returned.

Shahid, who had tried to pay his way out of doing stag on FIRST ENCOUNTER, managed to misplace his gas mask. As the CS gas circulated through the room, his eyes started to sting and his throat filled with the vile toxin. Unsurprisingly, he panicked, grabbing the nearest gas mask he could find, which happened to belong to Officer Cadet Hammond. Shahid was now fine. Hammond, however, having acted with even less haste than Shahid, was in a world of misery and confusion. He reached for his gas mask case, but found nothing inside. In his disorientated state, he couldn't identify the culprit.

More pressing still, there were two excitable colour sergeants, one Irish, the other Scottish, hovering over his shoulder analysing his movements, shouting that a village somewhere had been deprived of their idiot. Hammond couldn't hold his breath much longer. Tears streamed from his eyes. The pain was intense but he was stranded. He had no option but to flee the scene. He covered his mouth with his jacket, closed his left eye and ran outside before spluttering his way to a standstill.

The fallout was a true spectacle as a furious Hammond confronted an unapologetic Shahid, the rest of us standing a safe distance back. Shahid's actions reminded us of the joke about what to do if you and a friend are being chased by a lion and the response, 'I don't need to outrun the lion, I only need to outrun you.'

After an overpowering assault, we were outnumbered and forced into a hasty withdrawal from our gritty urban AO. This meant we were back to the unforgiving Welsh hinterland with three days of rural operations before a final assault to retake 'our' village. It was back to the familiar-ish routine of planning, writing and delivering orders, battle preparation and conducting recce patrols under the cover of darkness. Sandhurst places huge emphasis on your ability to operate at night, in order to utilise the principles of discretion, stealth and surprise. The British Army's ground operations during the Falklands War were a great example of this approach being put into action effectively.

Hammond's CBRN panic was far from the only incident of the exercise. Victorian Grandad – a keen high performer – was woken at 0200 and informed there was a Company Orders Group in 15 minutes: a set of orders delivered by the actual company commander, Major Stevens, to the temporarily appointed platoon commanders of 39, 40 and 41 Platoons in a small green tent near the harbour area. The orders needed to be taken down precisely. Crucially, they covered the company commander's mission and intent. It was then up to the person in command to digest that information and go through the Seven Questions process to come up with a plan before delivering their orders to the platoon and putting it in action.

Victorian Grandad wriggled out of his green caterpillar, put on his boots, helmet, webbing and rifle. It was chucking it down. He was, in Colour Sergeant Campbell's words, 'wetter than an otter's pocket'. Without additional light in the woodblock, he tentatively held his arms out in front of him before reaching the 'track plan' – chest-height string that connected all the shell scrapes to one another – then followed it to the stag position. He knew the OC's tent was close but he couldn't see it. He squinted his eyes and walked out from the harbour area in a direction that felt right. It wasn't.

He checked his Combat Casio. The O-Group had started. His heart was pumping and he wasn't thinking clearly. His walk turned into a trot and then a gallop around the dark woodblock in the pouring rain, unable to find the tent or his own harbour area. Discreet movement had been all but forgotten as serious anxiety set in. He wasn't where he was meant to be. Within seconds of getting his map out, rain rendered it useless. He stumbled from tree to tree. Seconds turned to minutes. No sign of life, just rain, darkness and trees. He stumbled some more.

'STOP! Advance one and be recognised.'

He tentatively moved forwards.

'State your name and purpose.'

'Officer Cadet Fyfe, 41 Platoon... I don't know where I am.' He felt ill just saying those words.

'STOP!'

In those few seconds, something inexplicable happened. The sentry of 37 Platoon Imjin Company, located almost five hundred metres from the 41 Platoon harbour area, decided to open fire. In real life, Fyfe would have been dead. In Sandhurst life, firing blanks, he wasn't. Instead, on pure instinct, he fired back.

'CONTACT!' the sentry duty yelled out and the drowsy members of 37 Platoon woke hearing that horrible word. All they could see was the flash of Fyfe's muzzle. The only sound was that of him firing. Fyfe didn't stop. With his adrenaline spiked, he changed magazine and continued to fire and move as a whole platoon fired back at him. He then tripped, fell and somehow became disconnected from his rifle. He continued to be fired upon but had no weapon to fire back with. Pure unadulterated panic set in. He turned on his headtorch. White light. He then yelled, 'I SURRENDER!' Before he realised what was happening, a pain drove into his ribs. He was on the ground again with someone on top of him with their knees by his shoulders.

'WHO THE FUCK ARE YOU? WHAT'S YOUR NAME? ANSWER ME!'

'Officer Cadet Fyfe, 41 Platoon. I'm lost. I'm sorry.'

It took a section of disgruntled members of 37 Platoon to assist in finding Fyfe's rifle before he was escorted back to our harbour area with his tail firmly pinned between his legs. The following morning, the escapades of Officer Cadet Fyfe spread like wildfire. As expected, the story escalated wonderfully to involve gas masks, grenades and a coordinated capture-the-flag-type kamikaze assault orchestrated by the Bear. Upon even the slightest mention of this tale in the times ahead, Fyfe's own tail would return to how it had been that night.

Map-reading, and getting lost, are part and parcel of the Army leadership game. Officers are notorious for it. To defend those with a commission – a nuance missed by their soldiers – officers are usually the only ones doing the navigating, thus absolving all others of potential accountability. There is also no denying that getting lost when leading ten soldiers, let alone 100 or more, is a real stomach-turner. At Sandhurst, using a GPS was banned. It was old-school map and compass, no fucking around. Given the outcry that occurred if the words 'I'm lost' were ever muttered, the greatest relief of any command appointment, second only to handing over responsibility to the next person, was simply getting to where you were meant to be going.

A fallout from this perpetual state of navigational fear during leadership was the necessity of conducting regular navigational (nav) checks. You can memorise the route on a map beforehand all you like, but when you're leading a patrol with DS hanging around, potential ambushes around the corner and a platoon of occasionally motivated, but certainly quite tired and irritable cadets behind, you need to make damn sure you get it right. They say that an army marches on its stomach, i.e. keeps its soldiers fed to sustain morale. They don't tell you that a quick way to sap the morale of your soldiers is to send them round the mulberry bush while you oscillate from north to south and contour to contour while also trying to identify your arse from your elbow.

Every so often, therefore, you stop to assess the ground, features and contours to identify your location. You hope you are where you think you are – internally, you're far from convinced. When doubt becomes overwhelming, features bear little to no resemblance to what you were expecting and the needle on your compass is pointing at right angles to what you plotted, you whip out the map and ask for other opinions.

Instinctively, you get your index finger and prod it towards your hoped-for position. The issue with an index finger on a 1:50,000-scale map is that its size places you potentially anywhere in a 500-metre area. Given that's roughly the range of an assault rifle, a wandering index finger is insufficient and potentially dangerous. Additional precision is required to pinpoint *exactly* where you are. So you, and those under you, kneel and analyse your immediate surroundings.

What you're looking for is a suitable pointer to use instead of your fingertip. You amass and discard an archive of grass, twigs and nearby foliage – just as Rafa Nadal selects tennis balls prior to serving. At this point, and only this point, post-getting lost, post-getting your map out, post-unsuccessful fingertip prodding, you can explain to others where you think you are, where you actually are and how you intend to get to where you want to be. And then you proceed towards your destination with your dignity intact. That is unless you double back on yourself, as happened to Norton on an elongated platoon patrol. There's no dressing that up – he must have wished the ground swallowed him whole and everyone's memory was erased.

Navigation was one of the essential military skills we learned. Others were first-aid training and mass-casualty responses.

Amputees in Action is an organisation that provides professional amputee actors for training simulations. These actors are often former soldiers, policemen and healthcare professionals who have sustained various injuries involving the loss of a limb.

During routine urban or rural patrols, we'd turn a corner and a high explosive grenade would go off followed by smoke grenades. The ensuing scene involved genuine amputees screaming, wailing and crying for help. There was fake blood, guts, torn clothing, mud, sweat and tears. It was a training scenario, but it felt authentic. A grown man, with a leg missing, calling out for his mum while gunshots were being fired nearby was the sort of thing that took you from imitation to reality. These scenarios forced us to respond in the most compassionate, pragmatic and logical way. Someone had to take charge.

A safety cordon was established to provide all-round defence. The platoon commander needed to send an immediate Contact Report to company headquarters. That transmission was a simple one: 'Contact, wait out.' It meant everything else on the net was stopped. That incident was *the* crucial scenario to be dealt with. The platoon commander then needed to assess the situation and relay the important information. Those in HQ were oblivious to the situation other than what was sent to them.

On the ground, each casualty needed to be attended to and triaged. Triaging is the process of sorting casualties into categories of treatment priority. Each casualty needed to be assessed on the severity of their injuries based on their communication and responses, the body parts affected, blood loss and breathing capability.

What followed was situationally dependent. The key was to convey to HQ what had happened through a full Contact Report – when, where, what had happened, what had been done and what would be done – or a 9-liner. A '9-liner' is a standardised format designed to convey an incident and prepare a suitable Medical Evacuation (MEDEVAC). It provides key information about the incident and the necessary evacuation procedures. Once you'd done this, the casualties were medically evacuated by car, helicopter or on a stretcher.

Situations were provided to give us a sense of what could happen and what we might need to be prepared for. You can't be prepared for every scenario but through our training, knowledge and understanding of the processes, our state of preparedness was increased. Our adaptability and flexibility to react to changing situations became one of our greatest collective strengths.

Some folk understandably froze to the point of utter incompetence when faced with these mass-casualty situations. As you were trying simultaneously to control your soldiers, listen to your radio, constantly assess the threat, understand the situation behind and ahead, know where the other platoons were, all while putting your own plan in place, Colour Sergeant Campbell tended to hover uncomfortably close and ask questions. 'Mr Stewart, just confirm, you, as the person in command, are unaware of how many of your men are *deed* right now,' he'd say. Or 'Mr Stewart, just confirm, half your platoon are combat ineffective, or *deed*, and you don't know the coordinates of the Helicopter Landing Zone (HLS).'

This line of enquiry, like a glance from the Medusa, was enough to turn the most attentive cadet to pure stone. Sometimes, too, it required every ounce of discipline you possessed to stop yourself from telling him to fuck off. As ever, he was probing, testing, teaching and assessing – small lessons as much as the big ones.

A genuine concern for many in CC133, and particularly 41 Platoon, was the fabled 'Backterm Hill'. Being backtermed was one of the worst potential scenarios for a cadet at Sandhurst. 'Backterm Hill' had developed a reputation as the burial ground of many a regimental dream, a place where visions of infantry heroism go to die and careers in organising vehicle moves are born. It also provided a key physical and mental test for those people struggling to cling onto the rhythm and tempo of the intake, helping them decide whether they were motivated enough to continue. It was a large nondescript hill in Wales, the kind we had gone up many times. But the long march up Backterm Hill came near the end of a heavy patrol and a long exercise when everyone's energy levels were depleted and each sodden step was one you'd rather not take. There was no enemy to face, just your own personal battle about how much you wanted it.

As the miles increased, the straps of your bergen began to dig uncomfortably into your shoulders while its base chafed the small of your back. The horizontal rain didn't help. The stopping and taking a knee as the guy in command appointment tried to navigate didn't either. Army terminology took a new turn as we learned the difference between being buggered and being fucked. The former, according to a South African in 40 Platoon, was a situation you could find a way out of, while 'being fucked... I mean, that's a whole different ballgame.' Being fucked was being, to use another bizarre phrase, 'man down shit pants'. Man down shit pants was the worst of the worst. It meant that physically, mentally, psychologically and emotionally you were a hopeless shell of your former self, a burden both to your own person and the people around you.

People followed the boots of the person in front knowing that giving up wasn't really an option. As rain lashed down on our sodden clothing, droplets trickled down our cheeks and our socks squelched with every step, we heard a vicious roar over-heard. With heads focused on the ground, our enthusiasm to look up was negligible. Three RAF fighter jets soared by in forma-tion before dipping their wings to pass by a second time. It was salt in the very open wounds of the grey folk ascending into the greyness. The Bear, up near the front, sensed waning morale and moved back through his troops, reminding us of his favourite mantras. 'Gentlemen,' he shouted over the wind, 'they're up there because they're not able to be down here. They can't do what you're doing. Not everyone can. Remember, it's not meant to be easy. If it was, everyone would do it. Keep moving and get to the top of this hill in good order.'

Maybe nobody needed to be told that they were unique for suffering, for enduring, but a few likely did. In the end, whether from RSB fears, loyalty to those around them or the sheer stub-bornness of not giving in, everyone from 41 Platoon managed to get to the top in good-ish order. We stopped, changed T-shirts and socks, had a bite to eat and were ready to move again. People's feet were blistered, their shoulders rubbed raw and their hands were cold. It was only after you'd finished these patrols that you realised the discomfort other people must have been in.

I retain an abiding memory of DRUID'S RIDGE, of something which occurred after our successful final attack. Thankfully it was successful. We conducted a recce patrol, marked the area for the rest of the company and then waited in the pitch black. Just waited. We couldn't speak and we couldn't (officially) sleep, although the scope on top of an SA80 made an excellent resting spot for the front edge of a helmet. We just lay shivering on the frozen grass feeling sorry for ourselves and painfully aware of the lack of sensation in our frozen fingers. We were waiting for sunrise. It seemed to take hours, the bloody thing refusing to rise from its slumber. Then when it eventually did pop over the horizon, we had to 'start sparking'.

The dawn assault was conducted with efficiency and a respectable level of professionalism. We encircled the village before methodically carrying out the commander's plan, moving from building to building safely, quickly and assertively. The shivering hours were forgotten and it was an enjoyable example of leadership and teamwork. My continued gratitude, and that of the rest of Falklands Company, must go to the ever empathetic enemy, Gurkha Company Sittang. Those soldiers had the good grace to grant us a safe reconquest of the village we had ruled for a forgettable three days.

It was after our temperate hollow square debrief that the incident I remember so clearly occurred. The endorphins were flowing, morale was high and the end was nigh.

After each of the Seven Questions in the Combat Estimate, you are meant to ask, 'Has the situation changed?' This allows commanders to process new information and adapt their plan accordingly. As a cadet at Sandhurst, you quickly learn that the situation often changes without warning and seemingly without reason. It's the 'hurry up and wait' syndrome. Sometimes, when things are bad, as they were on FIRST ENCOUNTER, you wish the situation would change and it doesn't. Equally, when things are good, as they were now, post-debrief, you don't want the situation to change and it does.

Which it did when we were told it was time to pick up the brass. 'Picking up the brass' is collecting used ammunition post-exercise from where you operated. It's a morale-sapping and seemingly never-ending process. However many empty 5.56 rounds you discover from years of exercises gone by in that dreary concrete FISCH setting, more appeared. It was a losing game of whack-a-mole. At some point, though, you realise you can't fight your situation. You have to accept it, be at peace with it and get on with the job at hand.

So instead of whack-a-mole, while picking up discarded ammunition in empty cold buildings and putting it in a heavy hessian sack, I thought of how Winston Churchill, Tim Peake, James Blunt and princes William and Harry must have felt doing this during their Sandhurst training experiences. It made me feel better. And then we heard those two beautiful words: 'STOP!' and 'ENDEX!'

And maybe, just maybe, beyond the command appointments, gassing, recce patrols, getting lost and overnight shivering, the real takeaway from DRUID'S RIDGE was just that. It was the internal thought process: embracing the contrasting emotions, accepting the concept of 'hurry up and wait' and understanding the shared moments experienced by every soldier, regardless of rank, at some point in their training.

⌒ — ⌒

Despite our minds being distracted by the upcoming regimental selection process, which was due to take place in a fortnight's time, life at Sandhurst plodded on.

Within clearly defined Sandhurst rules, we were given additional flexibility. Our competence now thankfully wasn't judged by the shininess of our door handles or the stencilling on our water bottles. Captain Connolly's room inspections still happened, but they often involved odd requests, such as keeping our doors open and adding more character to them. We were encouraged – or told, rather – to exchange the Army-issue blue duvet cover for one of our own. We were also strongly encouraged to bring in photos of family and friends and adorn the walls of our rooms with posters and pictures.

As part of Captain Connolly's open-door policy designed to foster inclusion, he became fixated on creating an atmosphere where the smell of roasting coffee beans wafted through the lines. With this newfound freedom to personalise our rooms, and as a means of maintaining alertness and helping us get out of bed, many of us acquired coffee-making apparatus. Our morning alarm was often followed by an outstretched arm switching on our Nespresso machine to somehow provoke forward bodily movement in spite of a refusing mind.

In this new, permissive era, we removed our original Sandhurst door signs, replacing them with satires of each other that cut dangerously close to the bone. We pooled our money and bought a Time Crisis arcade game machine to go in the laundry room, which required immense logistical effort but was worth it for the sense of silliness and autonomy it brought. We stretched cellophane across the Commodore's door before shouting, 'On the Line!' and watched him wrap himself up. There were other childish things that occupied our down time: taking advantage of people's unlocked rooms to hide their things, turning rooms upside down, wrapping them in kitchen foil, labelling every-thing or switching it from one person's room to someone else's. Returning from a medical appointment or a weekend away was always a nervy time.

Though still wary, we were more comfortable with our surroundings. The fears of marching incorrectly, accidentally saluting without a beret on or saluting a sergeant major instead of a major – both have crowns on their rank slides – were things of the past. We'd adapted to various other Sandhurst ways of doing things too, such as never wearing your beret inside. Ever. Even trips to the NAAFI for coffee had a typically Sandhurst feel. Without time to sit in and drink it – this *was* Sandhurst, after all – a takeaway was the only choice. At Sandhurst, however, one does not simply march with a Costa cup in one hand. There were two solutions: decant your cappuccino into a flask, or put the Costa cup into a plastic bag. Then you'd exit the NAAFI, put your coffee down while you replaced your beret, pick up your coffee again and march back to the signals wing with your right arm shoulder-high and your left arm rigidly by your side clutching your beverage of choice.

In and amongst the daily goings-on – the revising of regi-mental histories, the late-evening escapades and the fleeting visits to London to see girlfriends – we started to do more hypothetical battle planning. These are known as 'Tactical Exercises Without Troops' (TEWT) and was part of our Seven Questions training. They culminated not just in tactical and leadership analysis of Damian Lewis in *Band of Brothers* and Tom Hanks in *Saving Private Ryan*, but also led to an exercise called NORMANDY SCHOLAR that took us to northern France.

The planning phase for NORMANDY SCHOLAR started at Sandhurst. We were given historical maps and written orders to analyse as though it was 1944 and we had been promoted to play the role of commander of the British forces orchestrating the D-Day landings and airborne deployments. After a bus ride to France, during which we were entertained by classic Second World War films such as *A Bridge Too Far* and *The Dam Busters*, we were taken to the actual parachute drop points to give us context of how our plans might have unfolded. The reality of defensive anti-aircraft weapons protecting France and midnight parachute drops deep into enemy terrain meant plans were rarely conducted as hoped. The old Army adage of 'Improvise, Adapt and Overcome' came to mind for those brave soldiers deployed.

Our journey continued as we stood at the landing points on Gold and Juno beaches and tried, almost absurdly, to imagine what it must have been like for an 18-year-old second lieutenant coming ashore in the face of German opposition. Even for the most imaginative, standing there as fit and healthy officer cadets in clean British Army uniforms on a quiet spring afternoon on an empty beach, it was all but incomprehensible. We were so far removed from what had happened at that exact point on 6 June 1944 during Operation Overlord as shells went off, machine guns rattled, men wailed in agony and friends were shot. But it made us think.

Following the D-Day landings, Allied troops fought their way across the flat lands of northern France. Accordingly, we moved to planning assaults on nearby towns and coordinating defensive locations in village churches. At each position, we were given the task of being the commander and choosing a course of action, having gone through the Combat Estimate and the Seven Questions. What would we do? Where would we go? How would we react? The historical experts accompanying us then explained what occurred all those years ago. The exercise brought to life the planning processes we'd been taught. Sometimes we were given just a few minutes to adapt to new information and prepare a response. Other times we might have 30 minutes to prepare orders having understood many more of the potential constraints, limitations and opportunities that existed.

Our minds and imaginations, even aided by the accounts of experts, were insufficient. To truly understand, we needed to hear about it from someone who had really felt that adrenaline, terror and responsibility. That's what took us to Hill 112.

Unimposing, yet dominating the surrounding landscape, Hill 112 stands southwest of Caen. It had been captured and lost during Operation Epsom in June 1944. On 10 July, the Allies launched Operation Jupiter with the aim of recapturing the hill and further tying up German forces. Hill 112 was not the most famous of Second World War battles, nor the deadliest, but its significance cannot be overstated. General Hausser, a high-ranking commander in the Waffen-SS, called Hill 112 'the key to the back door of Caen'. Similarly, Erwin Rommel declared that whoever held Hill 112 held Normandy. The battle for Hill 112 took ten weeks of fierce fighting and cost the lives of around ten thousand men but doing so allowed the Allies to retake Caen and continue the liberation of Europe.

As part of the 43rd (Wessex) Infantry Division, Major John Majendie was the company commander of S Company for the 4th Somerset Light Infantry. Now aged over 90, Major Majendie met the 190 officer cadets of CC133 at the base of Hill 112. It was almost 70 years since he had stood there the same age as us in command of more than 100 young men tasked with assaulting and capturing the hill before us. Just as standing on Juno beach required boundless leaps of imagination to comprehend what it *could* have been like, the same sentiments were felt at Hill 112. There we were in pristine clothing complaining about the wind affecting our ability to write notes. Nothing, surely, could ever put us in the shoes of someone who had been as hungry, tired, pressured, motivated, determined, scared and brave as the man in front of us. How could we begin to ask him what it was like?

We took the same bounds up the hill as he had taken and tried to imagine how he might have gone about commanding his troops and delivering his orders. And then at the top of Hill 112, he spoke and we fell silent. We stood and listened, respectful, deferential, grateful. He talked with clarity and honesty about something we could only ever understand through books and stories. But these weren't someone else's stories; they were his stories, his memories. They were his friends who had been shot, his blood that had been spilt, his shovel that had dug into the ground and he who had spent nights awake as German Panzers pummelled his friends with shell after shell. We tried to understand how it had felt, how he had known what to do, how he had directed his men and what the main difficulties had been.

'We didn't really have time to think. It was them or us. You fought for the men to the left and right of you. You also fought for those back at home.'

These were lines which you heard in Hollywood films, but that was his reality. Men like Major Majendie were the sort of soldiers, the sort of leaders, we all aspired to be: stoic, loyal, determined, resilient, courageous. For us, the experience was sobering and moving. Our sleep-deprived nights on FIRST ENCOUNTER, being cold, wet and tired on CRYCHAN'S and digging shell scrapes on DRUID'S RIDGE were put into context. What we were training for would never come close to what he had gone through. But what he had gone through, what they had all gone through, was how and why many of us were standing where we were at that time.

He told us that many of the men who had served their country alongside him at Hill 112 had since requested to be buried there. The tightness and bond forged between these men, likely rarely spoken about during or since, was so strong that, even all this time later, they never wanted to leave each other's sides. Theirs was the ultimate sacrifice.

⌒ — ⌒

Every person who goes up those Old College steps with their ironing board under their arm has an idea of what an Army officer should be. As training progresses, most set aside their pre-conceived notions as their relative strengths and weaknesses are revealed. Not everyone who kicks a football becomes Lionel Messi and not everyone who drives a go-kart becomes Lewis Hamilton. Equally, not every officer cadet is destined to attain legendary status and accumulate racks of medals. That realisation can be harsh and RSBs were the culmination of a robust process.

The Army is split into various job roles: Infantry, Royal Armoured Corps (RAC), Royal Engineers, Royal Artillery, Royal Signals, Army Air Corps, Royal Electrical and Mechanical Engineers (REME), Intelligence Corps, Royal Logistics Corps (RLC), Adjutant General's Corps (AGC) and Royal Military Police (RMP). I have used acronyms for some based on how they're referred to, but not all. There are others, but that's the majority.

Other than joining, the decision of where you serve after training is the most important one in the Army and, with almost five months of military training complete, we each had a better idea now than when we started.

Each part of the Army has its own identity, history, ethos and mentality. One is not better than another (though of course, it's fair to say most regiments think they're better than the others) but you soon begin to understand, through research, rumours and conversations, where *you* might fit best. As you're made painfully aware, your regimental family – confusingly they all claim to be 'family regiments' – will stay with you forever.

Choosing your regiment begins before Sandhurst; even before AOSB, as you begin to understand different Army roles. In time, preferably post-AOSB but pre-Sandhurst, you go on an official regimental Potential Officer (PO) visit. There is no typical PO visit but the purpose of each is the same: for the regiment to sell itself to you, and for you to sell yourself to the regiment. It's an extensive and thorough job interview and character assessment. Arguably, your time at Sandhurst could be similarly described.

Regiments are allocated places per year based on their size. The most competitive ones – particular infantry and cavalry regiments – have only one or two places per intake. This means you're in direct competition with each person who is eyeing up the same position. This could be the same person you're in a room next door to or alongside in a shell scrape.

Each regiment wants to recruit the best officers and makes the impossible claim they only recruit cadets of the highest calibre, despite the obvious logistical and mathematical issue if this policy was adopted by all. Each regiment needs their officers to be flexible in thought, fit and resilient as well as self-motivated, disciplined and sociable. You're influenced by your friends, instructors, parents, fellow cadets, films, books and histories. You must establish your own priorities from the fellow officers, the job role, the recruiting catchment area, the uniform, the stories, the outside perception and your gut instinct. Your ego and competence must also align.

You wear uniform to show you're part of the British Army; you wear the individual quirks of your regiment to differentiate you. It's the name on your rank slides, the cap badge on your beret and the identity through which people immediately bracket you. The officers you serve with will be in framed pictures in your downstairs bathroom, ushers at your wedding and bearers of your coffin. The decision, therefore, really matters. As with university choices, or the Sorting Hat at Hogwarts, you learn to understand what certain regiments are looking for, whether you're right for a particular one and whether it's right for you. You might admire the ambition of Slytherin, the bravery of Gryffindor or the wisdom of Ravenclaw but are more suited to Hufflepuff.

Stereotypes can also influence. The line infantry hate books without pictures. The Parachute Regiment are chippy about the Marines and overly obsessed by their masculinity. The cavalry and Guards regiments are from private schools. The Royal Artillery failed to get into the cavalry or Guards. The Royal Tank Regiment (RTR) are known as 'Chav Cav'. Joining the Royal Military Police (RMP) begs the question of why they didn't save themselves a year of Sandhurst and join the actual police. Royal Engineers failed to get a civilian engineering job while the Royal Electrical and Mechanical Engineers (REME) failed to get into the Royal Engineers. Every regiment that isn't Combat Arms – infantry or cavalry – are called REMFs: Rear Echelon Mother Fuckers. Royal Signals, Royal Logistics Corps (RLC) and the teachers and admin officers in the Adjutant General's Corps (AGC) receive the brunt of the mockery.

And then there are the regimental mottos: The Rifles: 'Swift and Bold'; The Royal Lancers: 'Death or Glory'; The Light Dragoons: *'Merebimur'* ('We Shall Be Worthy'); Royal Engineers: 'First In Last Out'; Royal Gurkha Rifles: 'Better to die than to be a coward'; Coldstream Guards: *'Nulli Secondi'* ('Second to None'); Parachute Regiment: *'Utrinque Paratus'* ('Ready for anything'); Royal Signals: 'Swift and Sure'; Adjutant General's Corps: *'Animo et fide'* ('With resolution and fidelity'); Royal Logistics Corps: 'We Sustain'; and so on. Some will inspire, and some won't.

Even before day one, week one of training, and all the way until RSBs, egos were damaged and hopes were dashed as regiments cut people from their books. It was called 'getting chinned'. It was demoralising for the person involved as they went back to the drawing board, got out their black-ink cartridges, lightly drew a two-centimetre margin on their A4 writing paper and began chatting someone else up. Some changed course of their own accord – if neither the glove fitted the hand nor the hand the glove, it wasn't worth forcing it – while others were stopped in their path.

For some, the moment of truth might have been when they were shivering uncontrollably in the prone position with numb fingers, unable to read a map. It might have been when soaking wet, sitting under a tree, feeling sorry for themselves and trying to write orders. For others, it might have been when their body collapsed under the weight of their bergen or they received a strongly worded suggestion from the DS.

The decision for many was made during one nerve-wracking interview. We donned a suit, polished our shoes and straightened our tie. Given AOSB Briefing and Main Board, the written correspondences, the PO visits and the rigours of Sandhurst, just getting to this stage and still being in consideration was a positive. But the final outcome would be determined by the assessors in that room. For some, it was tea, biscuits, a pleasant conversation and a short confirmation of a predetermined acceptance. For others, it was analysis of regimental history, battle honours and Victoria Cross winners alongside abstract-reasoning tasks, watched over by a selection of senior soldiers and high-ranking officers. For all, it was a sigh of relief to leave the room.

RSBs determined a cadet's fate and the cap badge that they would be forever aligned to. People were put through the emotional wringer as tensions and nerves were heightened across the intake. There were high fives and hugs just as there were tears and locked doors. Getting accepted made you euphoric; getting chinned left you hollow. For those accepted, the days, even years, of hard work were worth it as your future cap badge became a certainty. For the rest, those whose first and second choices did not extend beyond final interviews, recalibration was necessary. As with university choices, you went to clearing and, with the background help of your platoon and company commanders, a home was found. Sometimes it was a realigned success story. At other times, an unsatisfying compromise.

It was a drawn-out procedure before getting a nod of approval or shake of the head. Not everyone is right for every role. Within 41 Platoon, there was an emotional spectrum representative of the intake: excitement for some at joining the same regiment but despondency for others as career paths diverged. Regardless of the outcome, it finally provided much needed clarity about our futures but would take time for the dust to settle over the remaining fortnight of Inters and beyond.

Chapter 8

'Mr Stewart, you'd be out of your depth in a car park puddle!'

We had just returned from a much-appreciated fortnight of leave, a blessing after the stresses of Inters and the accumulated toll of training. It had been sunglasses, sea and sand for some; running, rowing and reading for others. The fear of another personal fitness assessment soon into Senior term was enough to motivate some to lace up their trainers while an RSB capitulation ensured others lay discontented on their sofa. Some rekindled old romances while others tried desperately to sustain relationships hanging by a thread from the strain of Sandhurst. It was clear which cadets had suffered disappointment in love during the break, as they returned with a cigarette in hand – new, post-break-up smoking habits were not uncommon occurrences.

Now, instead of lying on the beach, watching the football at a pub or lazy Sunday mornings with a girlfriend, we were back at Camberley Technical College with colour sergeants Campbell and O'Sullivan reminding us of our mutant-like tendencies and puddle-coping capabilities.

Nobody in 41 Platoon wanted Exercise SENIOR STRETCH, a shake-out exercise designed to rid ourselves of our civilian cobwebs. A shake out in the sense of what a kid does to a snow globe's tranquil festive scene – Sandhurst's way of reminding you who's in charge – as we reacted to commands and wished we were elsewhere while feebly attempting to write orders under a basher in the rain using red light.

The final term was called 'Hotel Seniors', based on the privileges afforded, and the additional emphasis on individual development. Greater focus was placed on self-analysis and coaching rather than being taught. The Mars training had become increasingly specific, the Minerva training more significant.

There was a post-regimental Sorting Hat lull. People's motivation to commission was still a rollercoaster of peaks and troughs but that enormous elephant had (not very silently) exited the room. What remained was those vying for the top seeking the hardest command appointments and those at the bottom grateful that they might still complete the course. The ever-expanding middle third muddled along, content with their destination, content, too, that they would be standing on the parade square in 14 weeks' time if the boxes were ticked.

Exercise BROADSWORD was anticipated, revered and feared in equal measure. It was yet another rite of passage, but a more mature, complex and realistic one. In preparation for deployment, our focus was on riot training with face masks, 1.5-metre plastic shields and batons. We learned to form disciplined ranks, move according to set formulas, defend and attack with precision and controlled aggression as well as cope with firebombs, foreign objects being thrown and external assailants. Beyond the intensity and sweat-inducing thermal coveralls of riot training, we also studied the multifaceted aspects of modern warfare from Northern Ireland to Afghanistan to bring with us into the exercise. These conflicts weren't conventional wars of goodies versus baddies; they were complicated, nuanced and problematic.

The exercise was split into three phases: rural, urban and civilian population (CIVPOP). The scenarios involved IED-making factories, mass casualties, enemy encirclements and public-order control; deliberately intense pressure-building scenarios. And then there was the added scrutiny of instructors hovering over your shoulder asking the who, what, when, where and how questions while you were still processing the surroundings around you.

The first rural phase involved more than just red-versus-blue forces; there were neutrals, foreign forces, sympathisers, dignitaries, informants, translators, insurgents, unlawful combatants, resistant militias and asymmetric threats. We had multi-person mass casualties which required immediate first aid, triaging and evacuation. We had to act as a bridge between militias, the civilian population and local friendly forces. On each occasion, the orders process was longer and the questions harder. As well as using matchsticks to represent trees during orders, we used satellite images and dissected building schematics to assess potential entry points. We conducted close-range recces and ambushes. In conventional warfare – the initial part of our training – the answers had been clear and the scenarios fixed, so leadership flexibility was minimised. The answers were now ambiguous as we morphed into more complex warfare with greater scope for freer thinking.

The final two phases are what people remember best: urban and CIVPOP. Imjin Company began as soldiers working in an urban environment while we, Falklands Company, were CIVPOP. Our roles would subsequently reverse – there were pros and cons to each. We'd have a mid-exercise break from tough soldiering before reverting to uniform and cam cream. The inter-company rivalry provided an important thread.

The urban environment was like an abandoned ransacked village: rows of grey concrete houses without windows, doors hanging from their hinges, no furniture or amenities, just shells of two-storey buildings next to one another. There were railway tracks and grassy patches and a wooded area just off the main row of houses. It was all derelict, like something out of an apocalypse movie, except that unlike an apocalyptic scene with signs of life gradually removed, here it was as though nothing had ever existed. It was pre-catastrophe, as though something had been built and then forgotten about without any human traces – except empty blank rounds dotted about, the odd scrap of rubbish from a ration pack caught in a fence and a rogue scribble on the wall of a house. For Falklands, these empty buildings would become temporary homes. We spread ourselves about, unfurled our roll mats and, for the first time on exercise, even adopted that much-dreamt-about concept of boots-off gonkers. It was nap time with a bonus: the genuine opportunity to rest the eyelids without the DS interrupting you. Nap time without boots and socks on, without stag, an O-Group or being bugged out.

We showered, cleaned and ate while wearing civilian clothes to represent our pre-designated roles, which ranged from radical clerical leaders to shop owners, informants to double agents. Imjin were still in uniform, still dirty, still in cam cream and patrolling around the village. Being CIVPOP was living the dream. We were smugness personified as we sat outside in the sun, read and laughed while the other company 'observed our pattern of life' having left their Forward Operating Base (FOB) several times per day.

As CIVPOP, we escalated the pressure in accordance with DS direction. Rather than being meek, observant and rule-adhering, we were encouraged to goad, provoke and incite. We got up close and personal to the patrolling troops, tempting them into reacting and losing their control. We lured them in and urged them forwards. We turned the screw. We used chalk to write on the pavement and target certain people. We tried to isolate, encircle and panic individuals or patrols. We accepted the odd baton strike as punishment if we got it wrong but it was worth it for when we got it right. We learned little tricks to get under their skin: undoing their rifle slings, blurring their rifle sights, undoing their laces or disconnecting their radios. Our aim was to disrupt. Theirs was to move together and remain composed, controlled and disciplined. We used water guns to spray people on guard duty and mocked them for wetting themselves, knowing they couldn't react properly. Almost no patrol ran smoothly, as we somehow caused disorder every time.

Many of us were masked up and unidentifiable. We could pretend to be someone else, someone troublesome and unruly, which was both liberating and fun. For most, there was an element of acting, of genuinely testing Imjin in the knowledge that a) the roles would be reversed shortly and b) it was an exercise where we were all in the same boat heading towards to the same destination. On the other hand, some saw it as an opportunity to unleash a hurtful aggressive side. It was concerning to see the speed with which friends turned against others and flicked a switch in their head to cause harm to fellow cadets, who just happened to be in another company. The line was a fine one.

After the reviews and briefs, the roles were reversed. Imjin inhabited our abandoned houses, washed, wore civilian clothing, ate well, read and sunbathed while we feebly relocated our bergens, cam cream and rifles and took over their FOB. We learned from their soldiering errors and strengths. It was now our radios being tampered with by unidentified individuals while we enviously watched them doing yoga and laughing.

We had learned from studying previous conflicts that, for patrolling soldiers, posture is key. Arrive with tanks and machine guns and you won't be received with open arms by locals. The aim of winning 'hearts and minds' is achieved by de-escalation and relationship building. We patrolled first with our berets on

– soft posture – to understand the local dynamics. We needed to know the ringleaders, sympathisers and troublemakers among the population. The escalation process was meant to be incremental. Having been restrained in uniform, however, Imjin escalated fast, an understandable avenue for their built-up tension. We subsequently responded by prematurely moving to helmets, batons and shields.

The instructors scaled it back as tensions rose and escalation procedures were not adhered to. We now understood how it felt not knowing your opponents, yet feeling the force of their attacks, the anxiety as they attempted to kidnap us, the disturbing sense of being aware that *something* is going on but not knowing what, the internal conflict between wanting to react assertively and knowing this was a battle of personal discipline.

Still, our 'friends' in the other company felt less like that; they were rioters, protestors and campaigners. They sought to embarrass us and make us fail, as we had with them. As they encircled and attacked, we felt the gratification of smashing unruly rioters with batons, shouting, 'GET BACK!' before advancing forwards as part of an organised unit. As they sought fault lines, our riot-control procedures were methodical and structured. With that unity came power. We had to remember our training. Some managed well, others, as before, saw red, lost control and reacted rashly while others again backed off or froze.

Leadership came to the fore as we tried to cope with uncertainty. Colour Sergeant Campbell explained how our role as officers often involved putting reins on snarling dogs – those dogs being our soldiers, who wanted to close with and kill the enemy. As platoon commanders, we needed to understand the rules of engagement and the Geneva Convention as much as how to aim riot guns and handle high explosive grenades. We were there to control and protect those under our command, to keep our emotions from overpowering our rationality. Being a platoon commander for these scenarios was illuminating and demanding. In most scenarios at Sandhurst thus far, there was a course of action that you were *expected* to take; the *right* answer, in other words. Here, the right or wrong course of action was down to interpretation. Each decision-making process and outcome was a version of those many shades of grey.

Could you have advanced, called for reinforcements, withdrawn, escalated or appeased? Could you have taken a different route, adopted a different posture or better analysed personnel intelligence? Despite the grey shading, there were also erroneously crossed lines. People on guard incorrectly shot people they assumed to be insurgents with IEDs. Others, out on patrol, shot escaping rioters. Equally, some chose inaction and their fear of decision-making led to the encirclement and the capture of soldiers under their command. After each patrol, Captain Connolly and Colour Sergeant Campbell, who had been observing and listening, made us analyse, assess and learn in front of the platoon.

The consequences of those small errors were often anecdotally explained. Colour Sergeant Campbell recounted the impact of people he knew being captured by the IRA while on patrol, while Captain Connolly described post-Afghanistan retrospective legal cases based on the actions of his soldiers. This was still training, a safe space engineered for us to learn, make mistakes and fail in. The reality of what we were training for would be anything but. The scenarios were complex because our operational deployments would be complex. Our choices were scrutinised and the lessons disseminated because, in combat, you might not get a second chance, and we had to take on board all our collective experiences.

Baton strikes and bruises appeared with each new scenario. It all led to the final attack: our main test. Inside our FOB, we planned tactics, prepared kit and organised our order of battle. Outside the gates a crowd was gathering. What started as ten disgruntled individuals soon became a mob of 100 rioters armed with smoke grenades, flashbangs and firebombs and hammering on the gate. We had been the other side before trying to intimidate those inside. But it felt different knowing you had to go out. We were isolated. We were on the receiving end of thrown objects and threats. En masse they then left. Nightfall and quiet descended, and tension hung in the air.

We received a brief from Major Stevens telling us our plan and what we needed to do. The mood in Falklands Company was still somewhat muted. The Bear then stepped up and spoke, and the mood gradually changed. Although we knew that the fictional battle that awaited – Falklands versus Imjin – was a safe training scenario rather than genuine life or death, at that moment, as the darkness and silence spread and the walls of our FOB drew nearer, it felt like it really mattered.

The Bear's talk grew in vigour and fighting spirit. He knew there were no actual snipers, IEDs or ambushes waiting outside. There was no member of the Taliban trying to end the life of one of his 19-year-old soldiers. But, ever the professional, he understood the value of 'train hard, fight easy'. If it was easy, everyone would do it. He meant it. His talk was about going into uncertainty and trusting the person next to you. He spoke of discipline, focus and a warrior mentality.

He ended with a version of the Spartan call to battle from the film *300*. 'Falklands Company, what is your profession?'

Our response was clear and unified. 'HAROO! HAROO! HAROO!'

Nobody else could have pulled off such a potentially cringe-worthy final rallying call. But he somehow managed it. Even the cynical, capable and substandard cadets were riled up. At that moment, every one of us was ready to fix bayonets and charge over the top. We thought of Imjin waiting outside. They would have heard it and, by provoking their fear, our oratory power had a secondary impact.

We opened the gates and marched towards battle. In a most wonderfully British way, one of our men stood back and played the theme from *The Last of the Mohicans* on the bagpipes as we conducted our orderly but adrenaline-fuelled advance. We had shields, helmets, visors and batons. Smoke grenades were going off, objects were thrown at us and the only light came from fire pits that blazed in the inky darkness. The tension heightened as a few chancers attacked from the front.

'GET BACK!' Controlled aggression. The line advanced, struck the enemy with firm baton strikes and resumed its formation in our own fictitious version of the Spartans at the Battle of Thermopylae. Discipline. The lessons had sunk in. We remained in good order.

Wave after wave of attacks came crashing towards us as the front line was replaced by fresh bodies – some more willing than others to take their turn at repelling the charges. People were knocked sideways and backwards; fights broke out and sweat saturated the clothes we wore. Denser objects were thrown; more firebombs were directed at our feet to test our ability to stamp out the flames and remain orderly. Some tea bags, as ever, were stronger than others. At Sandhurst, you can't hide.

Hours later we returned to our FOB limping, sweating, exhausted, battered, bruised, beaten up and relieved. It had been several hours of complete focus, adrenaline and engagement followed by release. In the light of day, at breakfast the following morning, the grudging respect that existed between the two companies was evident. Like two heavyweight boxers who had slugged it out for 12 rounds before a split decision, there were no real winners or losers. The faces you knew nothing about two weeks before now appeared in brief flashbacks, with angry eyes, rapid baton strikes and genuine fear. As expected, shared stories of failure, humour, embarrassment and erroneous decision-making were the best of ways for us all to understand what we had experienced.

Returning from BROADSWORD as Senior term cadets with purple bruises, black eyes and a few broken limbs was another milestone. It was the same training so many had previously experienced when they too had plunged themselves into these scenarios. It was our first major exercise in our final term and now those in the intakes below were the ones asking questions and feeling envious as our Sandhurst days ticked by. More than the physical evidence, the characteristics required to excel were what mattered most. Avoiding being encircled required spatial awareness and swift decision-making. Avoiding losing your cool required discipline and composure. Advancing towards a confrontational crowd required bravery and teamwork. Lacing up your boots and patrolling alongside others in your platoon was indicative of the resilience, determination and endurance that is demanded of all soldiers at all levels. BROADSWORD had successfully lived up to its reputation.

⌒ — ⌒

Looking ahead, there was one last big exercise in Bavaria, DYNAMIC VICTORY, before the final countdown to the Commissioning Parade, our Commissioning Parade. With big tests, though, came casualties. Norton talked a good game – he even talked the talk – but walking was the issue. I mean that literally – he tended to get injured when the going got tough – but more specifically about walking the Sandhurst walk. The

Sandhurst bar is rightfully high – it is the standard you should want, and indeed need, to aspire towards. You're trained at Sandhurst to cope with uncertainty, make decisions and convey them to others – sometimes appearing calmer and more assured than you feel. You also learn the other stuff, the gritty, unseen, unlovable, unremarkable stuff. That's where the bar really is; it's not just the mesmerising set of orders at sunset. It is doing the right thing on a difficult day when nobody's watching. It is the standard you set and the examples you give. Not every person that heads to Westbury for AOSB is destined to be an Army officer, and nor should they be. Just as with RSBs, Sandhurst is selective while equally demanding brutal self-selection.

Sometimes people do slip through the cracks and emerge the other side. With eight weeks to go, two of which were on final exercise and three being the final camp farewell, we thought those who had made it this far would likely make it to the marquee at midnight. We were wrong.

Norton's talking and selective walking had been noticed early on by Colour Sergeant Campbell and Captain Connolly. He was on their radar. Unfinished exercises came and went, poor PFAs seemingly ignored and command appointments handled erratically. However, interspersed with that consistent inconsistency, there were moments of competence, of officerly potential. Cats have nine lives and Norton, it seemed, had more. As a platoon, we accepted that although he was not meeting the standard required, or expected, of a future officer, he would scrape through. BROADSWORD, however, appeared to be the final straw.

Captain Connolly resented Norton's course survival. On BROADSWORD, he witnessed Norton fire indiscriminately above a crowd and flee the scene leaving his 2IC to take over, before denying both acts had taken place, in spite of them being described by witnesses. For a commissioned officer, the punishment would be a court martial. For a cadet, it was less clear. Captain Connolly went berserk and wasn't discreet in sharing his feelings. 'It's a fucking joke' was the rough sentiment coming from this well-spoken officer.

Behind the scenes, the fallout set in motion a chain that led to a disciplinary meeting. Norton was not just backtermed to Inters or Juniors, he was kicked out of Sandhurst. With such a short stint ahead and a long run behind, it was a difficult decision, ultimately correct, albeit belated. The main justification was a failure of the core values of courage, discipline, respect for others, integrity, loyalty and selfless commitment. He was already on a final warning and had ticked all six boxes in one unthinking five-minute period.

Cookson-Smyth was a different scenario. His dad was an upward-looking major general and he was destined to join the same regiment – one of the most historic and traditional in the British Army. Being a confirmed cadet meant that his place was secured prior to starting at Sandhurst and he did not therefore go through the usual RSB process. If he commissioned, his place would be secure. The place offered could not be retracted without mutual agreement. It remains a controversial, some would say unjust, historic anomaly in the regimental selection process.

Cookson-Smyth's dad being a major general in the same regiment meant they were unlikely to retract the place and he was unlikely to give it up. But his performance was concerningly poor. For all his affability, there appeared an unbridgeable gap in skill and knowledge. This was *the* Cookson-Smyth who had been caught grilling his chest, having ironed his uniform while wearing it to save time, and discovered napping in the Portaloo on FIRST ENCOUNTER.

He must have been aware of his performance – his reports, dressing downs, warnings and show parades were evidence enough. Like Norton, he had had an unforgettable time on BROADSWORD. As platoon commander, he had allowed himself to get captured by the enemy. Like Norton, he fired erroneously into the back of an unarmed escaping rioter. His full riot-gear performance was concerning and, on multiple occasions, he escaped the front rank. In two months' time, however, he would earn his commission and join his regiment. We accepted it as a systemic failing and just one of those things.

One afternoon, with under two months of the course remaining, Cookson-Smyth missed a two-hour loaded march. The excuse of a sore lower back was hardly a surprise to the platoon who had heard similar reasons before. Having returned muddy and sweaty, we changed uniform for a lesson on the Law of Armed Conflict (LOAC) by Captain Connolly. Before the PowerPoint loaded, Cookson-Smyth knocked on the door in his Savile Row suit and Hermes tie. He explained why he'd missed the TAB and why his room was empty. He had made the decision to leave Sandhurst.

He said that joining the Army, in the same regiment as his father, and becoming a British Army officer, had been his dream ever since wearing his father's beret, putting on cam cream and camping in the garden as a little boy. He had never thought about doing anything else. He was proud to attend Sandhurst and truly wanted to stand alongside us on the parade square. But he knew he wasn't as good as he'd hoped. He knew he was an anchor on the platoon, holding back our forward momentum, and knew he wouldn't have earned his regimental place without being a confirmed cadet. As such, he felt it right to leave, to not pass go and not earn a commission. He said that he was grateful for our support and sorry he had not performed better, then wished us luck and said to keep in touch. He was close to tears throughout. He then left the room.

A prolonged silence followed his departure. Captain Connolly, to the point as always, said, 'Leaving this close to the end... says a lot. Wheat from the chaff. Let's crack on.'

The two departures – Cookson-Smyth's voluntary, Norton's involuntary – provoked intriguing platoon conversations. It gave us additional belief in ourselves and heightened the scepticism we felt about the system. For Sandhurst to maintain its reputation, and for officers to provide an example both to their soldiers and society of the core values of the British Army, the standard must be high. It's hard to want or expect the highest from those you command when you fall woefully short of that level yourself. Earning the respect of your soldiers – and it had to be earned – was tough to achieve. It was also extremely easy to lose. For two cadets to fall short of that mark was part of the Sandhurst filtering process. As Captain Connolly said, wheat from the chaff. The system worked.

However, for them to both reach the final furlong of their journey highlighted flaws in the process. If their performance was closer to satisfactory and the potential was evident, it might have been different. Norton had never even finished an exercise – he always appeared a round peg almost forced into a square hole.

We wondered whether Sandhurst telling Norton he wasn't up to it influenced Cookson-Smyth to pack it in. Maybe he feared that, upon commissioning, he might subsequently disappoint his father. Maybe, deep down, he knew it wasn't right for him and his embarrassment on BROADSWORD was simply the final nail in his coffin. Either way, as the platoon quickly pointed out, their departures opened up additional ticket invites to the Commissioning Ball for the rest of us.

As the scope of the course expanded and its complexity increased, we developed our skills as leaders and thinkers rather than as foot soldiers. Officers need to develop a comprehensive understanding of their environment, listening, conversing, thinking – condor moments – then acting. As a junior officer, you are not a section commander in charge of a fireteam, nor are you a trooper with a machine gun. Instead, you're orchestrating their movements, knowing when to stick or twist. We were learning the moral responsibilities of leadership, as opposed to just the smash and grab.

In the periods before and after exercises, we were in the academic hall. This department included War Studies, International Relations and Communication and Applied Behavioural Science (CABS). We learned about past and present conflicts and gave presentations on situations which provided moral tests of leadership: Bloody Sunday in Northern Ireland, Srebrenica, the Falkland Islands or Afghanistan. We analysed negotiation and influence strategies, persuasion techniques, British foreign policy, EU membership, NATO and toxic leadership. Each time, consciously or unconsciously, we had to think about how we would act in similar circumstances, what we would prioritise and what could have been done differently. We were taught problem-solving and decision-making skills, the nature of biases and effective communication methods.

When you take command of your soldiers, their problems become your problems. You have to understand each marital dispute, sick child, car crash, promotion course and sporting ambition. As a recently commissioned officer, you're forced to listen and learn. You need to find the answers to hitherto unencountered problems: credit card debt, gambling addiction, assault charges, course selections, stamp duty, PTSD, moving house, parental bereavement, long-term illnesses, job changes and demotions. None of these are exceptional incidents; many are everyday issues. Our learning at Sandhurst was not just box-ticking. It was integral to the lives of others.

Understanding the military successes of Slim, Montgomery, Wellington, Marlborough and Cromwell were important. Equally, studying the realities of war, as exemplified by Stalingrad, the Somme, Vietnam and Kosovo, was paramount to our education. Our recommended reading included obvious big hitters such as Sun Tzu and Clausewitz – it's hard to go anywhere in British Army leadership circles without hearing a quote from Clausewitz – but also books such as *Black Hearts*, about American troops in Iraq, showing how a lack of discipline and low-level leadership spiralled into atrocities being committed on civilians. Then there were books on leadership psychology and first-hand accounts. There were alpha male shoot-em-up stories, critical insights into foreign deployments and political memoires justifying erroneous decisions. They were all important, allowing us to learn from successes and failures.

Almost every lecture began with a version of 'It's an uncertain world out there, look at what's happening in country XYZ. In a matter of months, you *could* be deployed on operations.' We knew this wasn't likely but we smiled and nodded in agreement. We discussed and wrote essays on upstream conflict prevention, counterinsurgency campaigns and LOAC. We were repeatedly reminded of Von Moltke's maxim that no plan survives contact with the enemy, i.e. you can plan and plan again but it'll probably go to shit anyway. This was neatly summarised by Mike Tyson's 'Everyone has a plan until they get punched in the face.' Evander Holyfield's ears might be testament to that philosophy. We had media training by filming each other in mock-up scenarios and analysing the responses. We better understood the concept of mission command – centralised intent with decentralised execution, i.e. giving those under your command the freedom and opportunity to execute your orders to enable greater initiative and speed of action. We thought about the difference between leadership and management, the ability to follow and how to effectively work as a team.

In a peculiar episode, our company commander, Major Stevens, dragged us out of bed early to illustrate different command strategies. He got two cadets – both keen top-thirders – to say, 'Follow me' and walk away into the distance across playing fields. He asked whom we'd follow. Naturally, the majority went to the person they respected most. This was not the expected answer, so the exercise was tweaked. One then commanded, 'FOLLOW ME!' and powered off. The other said, 'Follow me' meekly and basically walked around in circles like a dog searching for its own tail. Upon being asked again whom we'd follow, we chose *Homo sapien* above canine. This appeared to satisfy Major Stevens, who contentedly explained that our leadership styles would have implications for those we led. With that advice delivered, he departed, and we left feeling more confused than before.

In the 21st century, the British Army's might is overshadowed by that of our competitors so we have adapted our approach. We're small but professional, limited in numbers but effective. We're not in the land-grabbing business but we influence where we can. David didn't beat Goliath on strength, but rather on guile. As such, we learned about the 'Manoeuvrist Approach': the indirect approach of applying your strength against enemy weaknesses, blending lethal and non-lethal actions to achieve your objectives.

This strategic approach was also adopted in tactical bursts, most notably by Shahid. Having previously tried to bribe Colour Sergeant Campbell on FIRST ENCOUNTER to get out of doing stag, he was consistent in his lack of passion for this activity. This was discovered post-DRUID'S RIDGE. Rumours did the rounds of £20 payments offered to other 41 Platooners to cover his late-night duties. His excuse when discovered: practical application of Manoeuvrist Approach principles, applying his strength against the enemy's weakness. It was a commendably quick response that temporarily muffled even Colour Sergeant Campbell's sharp wit.

We also learned about the OODA Loop – Observe-Orient-Decide-Act – developed by Colonel John Boyd of the US Air Force in the 1950s after his experiences dogfighting in the Korean War. The cycle begins with an observation which leads to a participant to orient on possible options before deciding on an appropriate course of action, and finally acting on that decision. At that point, the results are observed, and the cycle begins again. Success in the OODA Loop game means acting quicker than your opponent. The aim is to get inside an opponent's OODA Loop, break their rhythm and cause them to restart their observation. As a Sandhurst cadet, your OODA Loop is constantly targeted by your instructors seeking to force constant re-observation and subsequent (hopefully) amended action.

Then we learned *the* key takeaway about how to act as an officer. Step aside Churchill, Nelson and Lord Nolan's Seven Principles of Public Life, the real winner was known as the *Daily Mail* test: if the *Daily Mail* saw what you were doing, and filmed it, would it stand up to public scrutiny?

The leadership lessons were constant and self-evaluation was a reoccurring theme. There were expectations about doing the right thing on a difficult day when nobody was watching. We were told our soldiers wouldn't want us as friends, as they had those already. As a junior officer, you were not there to be liked; you were there to lead. Soldiers want their officers to be professional, competent, knowledgeable, fit, relatable and empathetic; they want to know you're a good person and that you'll look out for them. Senior officers often said we'd grow to love our soldiers during our time in command, just as they did. At other times, our instructors across all ranks politely and diplomatically reminded us that our soldiers didn't need our love, just as they didn't need our friendship. What they really needed was our leadership.

～ ～ ～

As the summer months arrived and the sunshine bore down on the cadets of CC133, our concerns were less about autumnal leaf-sweeping and unpleasant wintry exercises of Juniors and Inters and more about the Saturday afternoons of sport, before escaping to London and winning the first pint race. We had developed mature relationships with our instructors and were more confident with ourselves. At times, Sandhurst was – dare I mention it, for fear of future generations being denied such an occurrence – genuinely fun. We sent invites to family for the Commissioning Parade and friends for the Commissioning Ball. We had formal correspondences from our future regiments looking forward to welcoming us. Suddenly there was light at the end of the factory tunnel.

Despite being located near London, where Sophie lived, my relationship, like that of many others, was surviving by threads. The cancelled holidays, weekends and phone calls took their toll. In every spare evening slot in the hectic training schedule, once a week at best, I fled and drove hastily into London. I rarely used the sign-out sheet and hoped I wouldn't get found out. A few unexpected fire alarms and evening 'On The Line!' calls caught me out but there was usually someone to cover my back, just as I had done for them; that was platoon life. With light on the horizon, however, it also brought clarity about what the future might hold and what a life of service could entail. The reality was that, although Sandhurst was a bubble, a secluded anomaly in the career of a soldier, it was also the start of a longer journey. Ahead was a commission, deployments abroad, commanding soldiers and everything else the life of a junior officer encompassed.

I had spent the best part of nine months fighting my capture and seeking escape, wanting to keep something back for myself and not letting Sandhurst have everything. I resented Sandhurst a bit for denying me a chance to have a life outside uniform. Sophie provided a sense of normality, realism and compassion. With that normality also came the awareness of what the abnormality of military life entailed. The long distances, late nights, early mornings and cancelled holidays weren't just for now; they were the future, its length as yet undetermined: three years, ten years, 30 years. Neither of us knew. We spoke as often as possible, and we loved and laughed, but, one morning, I hastily arranged a fictitious 10 a.m. physio appointment in order to hop in my car and drive to meet her at a railway station. There, amicably and understandably, our relationship ended in sad tears; a mutual recognition that it wasn't meant to be. I guess I was now yet another bloody Sandhurst statistic. I decided I would hold off on the smokes for another few months so as not to tick all the clichéd boxes.

I was not alone. Many of our platoon had, or were having, similar issues in their own love lives, likely themes for the remainders of our Army careers. Unplanned deployments led to cancelled plans and unplanned duties led to cancelled dinner bookings. As ever, dark humour, the sharing of experiences and stiff upper lips were all part of our coping mechanisms. As much as Army life is tough for the individuals themselves, the fallout from their service has a wider, and less observable, impact on loved ones. It is another tier of commitment that the Army demands. The stories soldiers tell friends are often the positive ones, including funny situations, camaraderie and remote places. What others usually don't see is that each deployment is another period away from those you care about. It's a personal choice, a conscious and conscientious sacrifice, but one that is often overlooked. Each night in a barracks, or a ditch in a training area, is another night not spent with a partner. Each show parade or guard duty is another evening spent in uniform not cooking together and watching a film in the arms of someone you love.

Chapter 9

'WHAT MAKES THE GRASS GROW?'
    'BLOOD! BLOOD! BLOOD!'
    'WHAT IS THE BAYONET USED FOR?'
    'KILL! KILL! KILL!'

Taken in isolation, the scene is absurd. The 30 young men of 41 Platoon are stomping up and down on the spot in uniform with salty sweat dripping off their brows, each holding a single item: a rifle fitted with a bayonet. The bayonet lane is part of every soldier's training and so when the instructor asks us what makes the grass grow and what the bayonet is used for, we shout in unison, 'BLOOD! BLOOD! BLOOD!' and 'KILL! KILL! KILL!'

Upon the command of 'ADVANCE!', we charge forward in a row. Our faces aren't the innocent ones that arrived nine months earlier, those of unworldly young men unsure of how to iron their kit or lay out their room. These faces are maniacal, angry, psychotic. Rain lashes down as we grasp our rifles firmly in both hands. Like amateur hurdlers approaching a hurdle, we take a series of mini-steps to correctly judge our distance. We drive our rifles forwards, the movement full of aggression, with no holding back, no second thoughts. With a roar, almost a cry of anguish, we release our pent-up anger as we plunge our bayonets into sand-bags hanging from wooden scaffolds. The sandbag is the enemy.

'HIGH PORT. CHECK BAYONET. EN GARDE!'

I stand in the correct position, test the bayonet is still attached and get ready to move again. Even after this moment of high hostility, it comes back to discipline, before moving forwards, turning 180 degrees and continuing to stamp your feet into the ground while shouting that the blood makes the grass grow and bayonets are meant for killing.

One at a time, we're called out and removed from the group. An instructor I've not met before shouts directions about where to go. I have to run. My legs are heavy, my feet like lead. Puffing and panting I move.

'GET DOWN!'

I'm leopard-crawling on the sodden grass now. The grass turns to gloopy mud. I continue inelegantly, trying to move forwards with elbows and knees, but I'm going nowhere fast, sliding and soaking. There's barbed wire above me, inches from my face. I must stay low. I try to take a break but the yelling comes thick and fast: 'GET A FUCKING MOVE ON!' There's no pride on show here anymore as I wriggle along on my belly like the snake banished from the Garden of Eden. I stagger to my feet.

'ADVANCE!'

A sandbag appears before me.

'AHHHH!!!'

I unthinkingly plunge my rifle into another object. I'm sent running in a new direction. Up a hill, round a bend and over a wall.

'ADVANCE!'

Another sandbag.

'AHHHH!!!'

I plunge the bayonet deeply in once more. Another direction is assigned as I drag my exhausted body around the course. Into a stream, through a drainage tunnel and back under the barbed wire. A smoke grenade goes off, a high explosive grenade follows.

There's noise everywhere, my vision is impaired but there's still the instructor's voice: 'STOP FUCKING THINKING AND START FUCKING KILLING. ADVANCE!'

Another sandbag figure emerges out of the smoke.

'AHHHH!!!'

In a fatigued daze, I plunge the bayonet in once more. I'm on autopilot as the actual act I'm learning to do – driving a seven-inch piece of metal into another person – is beyond me. That act is so far outside my comprehension or desire that I can't let it enter my mind. Colour Sergeant Campbell often says that he's trying to make us steely-eyed dealers in death. It's said tongue-in-cheek but, knowing the future roles of some members of 41 Platoon, is laced with realism.

At Sandhurst, you train hard to fight easy; yet fighting does not come naturally. Despite the confusion, exhaustion and misery involved in dragging my carcass around with a rifle and bayonet through mud, sweat and rain, the exercise is also about showing discipline and courage. Every member of CC133 has the same motivation, whether Falklands or Imjin, man or woman, infanteer or signaller.

Each thrust of the bayonet is instantly followed up with a yell of 'HIGH PORT. CHECK BAYONET. EN GARDE!' It's not mindless aggression but rather controlled force. Some argue that the bayonet lane should be done in Juniors at Sandhurst as an introduction to responding to orders and to assess your mental strength under duress. In Seniors, however, you've developed the skills and knowledge to be able to listen to the orders, display the aggression and then, crucially, rationally, withdraw.

Before commissioning, various administrative, fitness and shooting qualifications needed completing. Days at the ranges were perpetual bullshitty DS games of metaphorical hurry up and wait. We always arrived late and at pace as the range instructors simmered with rage. The moment we stepped into their domain, we received the recurring message of 'You'll see me angry, and trust me, gents, you don't want to see me angry.' We'd have cofftea and range stew for lunch in the pissing rain while being informed that we were 'living the dream' and that 'civvies would pay thousands for this'. Just as the tepid stew was digesting, we'd be told to 'start sparking'. Despite the dampness, Gore-Tex jacket and trousers were forbidden by the infantry instructors who generously reminded us that our skin was waterproof and the enemy didn't care if we were wet.

If we didn't spark in the manner they intended, or didn't shoot as straight as they said they could, or didn't relax our muscles while lying in the prone position in the rain while some angry Brummie colour sergeant ordered our bodies to remain motionless, we received what they referred to as 'free phys'. Rather than cadets, we became horses that bookies (the DS) could place wagers on as we conducted our own versions of the Grand National, running between and climbing in and out of the firing trenches. With our heart rates suitably spiked, our vision blurry from the moisture and our morale sapped, the instructors still couldn't understand why we didn't correctly adopt the 'Marksmanship Principles' of creating a steady position and controlling our breathing. And so the cycle continued with more jumping, more hurrying, more waiting and even some shooting thrown into the mixer for good measure.

With the face-paint-and-command-appointments side of the course almost completed, we spent a huge amount of time learning about Joint Service Publication (JSP) 101, which is the military writing guide. This document is the reason all military documents are, theoretically at least, formatted the same way and in the same language. It's the reason our first encounter on FIRST ENCOUNTER was, or was not, capitalised. It's the reason that, in any documents, the font and margins are the same, the dates and times are standardised and known as 'DTG', which stands for 'date-time group', and there are two spaces after every full stop. There are clear benefits to this rigour but learning it is painful for all involved.

Some people excelled. The Commodore, credit to him, was one. It wasn't excelling as Sandhurst would publicly endorse – integrity, leading from the front, doing things the right way – but the Commodore knew people who knew people, and thus he procured someone else's template and with it learnt how to swiftly complete all written tasks. We amended a version of his one, adjusted the dates and all jumped onto the next square together.

We also passed the Endurance Training Leader qualification which meant we could take our soldiers on a steady state run and stretch. For health and safety reasons, irrespective of our prior knowledge, anything beyond a steady state run and stretch was denied. We passed modules in Human Resources and Administration to prepare us for soldier welfare and personnel administration cases. To our pleasant surprise, our mere attendance and anticipated completion of CC133 meant that we were awarded with a Level 5 Extended Diploma in Management and Leadership from the Chartered Management Institute. When we invariably left the forces, we were reliably informed, the institute would provide necessary CV and LinkedIn fodder.

With the key components completed, and us deep into Hotel Seniors now, our attitudes shifted. The standard 'five minutes before' was shaved, second by second, until 'a few minutes before' became 'don't be late' and then 'don't be last'. Any blank space in the training programme was utilised by locking our doors, shutting the curtains, turning our platoon WhatsApp on mute and adopting the lights-off-sub-duvet-boots-off-horizontal-eyelid-inspecting position. The same could be said for our hour-long lunch period. The quicker the eating, the longer the napping. With PT less aggressive, breakfast remained optional for much of 41 Platoon who preferred counting sheep to a bowl of Corn Flakes and a soggy poached egg.

Midweek London ventures became more common. Cadets began to get into more trouble. For Officer Cadet Harris, 39 Platoon, a middle-ranking Royal Artillery officer in waiting, the draw of dating apps and London clubs was magnetic. Post-ranges, he bolted east to attempt to charm a trainee lawyer from Fulham named Tilly. In the wee hours, Colour Sergeant Thornton encountered him somewhat hazily heading up the staircase to his room. His justification? He asked Queen Victoria – the statue, that is – whether his overnight absence was approved. She kindly agreed that it was.

With a chapel parade early on Sunday morning, most people were having a quiet Saturday night in. Harris, at the AGM of the Academy rugby club, had other ideas. The dress code was blues, the smartest order of dress. The night started well with a few drinks, polite conversation and a few speeches. It escalated and Harris proceeded through the levels quickly and assertively. The buttons were undone, the shoes came off, the eyes glazed over and he soon went full Four Romeo with chanting, stumbling and chundering. While heading back, he took a brief and unplanned dip in the Sandhurst lake before being accompanied to the block.

Not many hours later, Harris was rudely awoken on his floor. His phone lay wet and broken next to him. His attire: blues, the fully sodden variety. Dress code for the most important chapel service of the intake: blues. Harris then had a choice: either stay put and manage the consequences, or head onto the parade square and blag his way through it. Against the advice of all, Harris plumped for the second option. His discretion was easy to miss as he swayed on the spot amongst an otherwise stationary platoon. The first man to survey the scene, and observe the puddle that had formed around Harris's feet, was, of course, the Bear. He promptly informed Harris that he was in a worse state than Mardirossoyan's post-exercise bergen, before having him chaperoned off with instructions to hide in his room.

By the Monday morning, the story had gathered snowball-like momentum and the truth was hard to decipher from reality. The result: his extra-curricular ventures were denied. He was restricted to the confines of the Sandhurst boundaries and he got rather used to shovelling horse manure at weekends rather than doing his best John Travolta impressions in average and over-priced London clubs. As punishments went, it could have been worse. A friend told me his dad had been ordered thirty years before to empty the dirty puddles on the parade square and refill them with clean water as a punishment. It was oddly reassuring to know that not much had changed.

From early in the course, two threats were regularly thrown at us beyond the usual show parades and weekend work parades. The first was returning the state of our rooms, and room inspections, back to day one, week one. The second was switching rooms with someone else.

With discipline sliding, and our lack of belief that these threats would be enacted, we continued to make parades on time rather than five minutes before. Our bluffs were finally called and the chickens came home to roost. Colour Sergeant Campbell enjoyed telling us our rooms were to move one place to the right and that a room inspection awaited us at 0700 hours the following morning. We groaned; but play with enough fire and you're going to get burned. Back to week one we went.

'Good morning, Colour Sergeant. 30158227, Officer Cadet Stewart, awaiting your inspection.'

'Good morning, Mr Stewart. And what a morning it is here in Senior term at the *Royal* Military Academy Sandhurst.'

'Indeed, Colour Sergeant, and what a pleasure it is for me to welcome you here.'

Campbell, I and everyone else knew that the DS were making a point, reminding us of who was in charge and that, even though we'd be commissioning soon, we were still officer cadets. His menacing grin reflected his enjoyment of our mutual rapport and situational awareness.

'Mr Stewart, what's that?'

'That would be my curtains, Colour Sergeant.'

'Aye, Mr Stewart. Why, at this glorious time of 0715 hours, are your curtains blocking this beautiful British sunshine?'

'I'm not sure they are, Colour Sergeant. They look pretty open to me.' The curtains were open, pulled back and fastened. I knew Campbell well enough to see how this script would unfold.

'Evidently, Mr Stewart, you think it's nighttime.' He drew the curtains to block the light. 'Seeing as it's dark, it might be time for you to get some sleep.'

'I'm not sure I'm that tired anymore, Colour Sergeant, but I appreciate the concern.'

'Aye, Mr Stewart, perhaps not, but it's a long day ahead so maybe sleep isn't such a bad idea.' There was only one way this was heading. I unpeeled my spotless duvet cover, before carefully getting into bed in my full uniform with my beret on.

'At attention.' I put the heels of my boots together and placed my hands rigidly by my side. 'Right, sleep well, Mr Stewart.'

Colour Sergeant Campbell turned the lights off, left my room and shut the door behind him. I could hear him then going in and out of other rooms complaining about whatever piqued his attention. In normal circumstances, this would be the sort of napping opportunity to wholeheartedly embrace but lying there at attention in my uniform, I wondered what to do next. How long was I to remain there? I couldn't get up, open the door and turn the lights on. So I waited. On his return walk, he came in and turned on the lights.

'Ah, Mr Stewart, I hope you had a nice lie-in while the rest of us have been at work. Good morning and welcome back to 41 Platoon.'

The show parades from room inspections came thick and fast – for the usual misdemeanours. We accepted our temporary defeats. On morning form-up, Lockwood received a Campbell show parade for 'showing wasp removed from face'; the little blighter took an ill-timed flight and went exploring around Lockwood's schnoz while he remained commendably calm. Campbell conducted 'the old cotton-wool test' on Russell and Victorian Grandad to assess whether they had shaved: in this you run a piece of cotton wool slowly from the top to the bottom of someone's cheek and neck and, if it catches, it is clear they haven't shaved properly. Russell passed with aplomb, a seamless flow across his ageless baby face. For Victorian Grandad, however, it was like falling from the top of a tree to the ground and hitting every branch en route.

Come 2100, Colour Sergeant Campbell's favourite time of day, the majority of CC133 had fallen foul of their colour sergeant's exacting standards. More than 150 officer cadets stood on parade. The opening brief concluded with the remark that the intake 'had more extras than Ben Hur'. It was an eclectic mixture of outfits, offences and corrections. Philipps had his whole bed out with him – showing bed springs with rust removed – while the Commodore had new water bottles, having been found with black polish on his original ones to cover the dirt. Lockwood showed his face without the wasp. Victorian Grandad had practically epilated his face in a valiant attempt to prove his shaving prowess. Lombard received a show parade for not moisturising correctly, having been informed that his face was 'drier than Gandhi's sandals'. He was ordered to 'Show moist', which he did by pouring a bottle of water over himself. Kieliszewski's show parade, displaying himself without an erection, was the result of his having previously been caught on parade with a bulge in his nether regions. A reshow for 'not standing straight to attention' was an inevitable follow-up.

⌐ — ⌐

With group PT sessions now a rarer commodity, the PTIs made each session count. It remained phys, it remained free and it remained stomach-churningly unpleasant. There was the race up and down a leg-burningly hilly cross-country running route on the training area called 'Five Ways'. It started on an intersection with, you guessed it, five tracks coming off it. As our hearts exploded and our legs refused to move, it successfully made us all question our life choices. There was also the Annual Combat Fitness Test – a 1.5-mile PFA route with full kit (around 15 kilograms) plus a rifle. The results were concerning in some ways as the leaders somehow managed to clock significantly quicker times with boots, a daysack, a rifle and combats than slower members of the platoon could on a normal PFA in shorts, trainers and T-shirt. Fitness evidently wasn't a priority for some.

We all passed our final mandatory weighted TAB. The weight we had to carry on these, and the distance we had to cover, had been incrementally increasing since Juniors. It had started with a couple of miles and around five kilograms. It ended closer to ten miles with a 25-kilogram load. A Sandhurst/PTI rule was that we were banned from using any 'dead weight', i.e. non-military-specific equipment. The issue with this rule was that we didn't usually have the weight in military-specific equipment in our rooms – a problem that grew as the required weight increased. Before each TAB, we'd go to the platoon store cupboard and sign out miscellaneous items such as entrenching tools, pickaxe handles, gaffer tape and body armour. When the cupboard was empty, we had to improvise with 'dead weight' from our rooms, such as gym weights and water bottles.

Usually, the weight was checked but the contents weren't. Until the final TAB. Our 41 Platoon PTI did a random check which caused panic and embarrassment amongst all present, when assorted items such as laminators, dictionaries, shower gel and shampoo were located. The ensuing punishment was for us all to have to swim in the Sandhurst stream in full uniform and use the dead weight as it was intended. The ensuing foamy lather provided a surreal, but likely necessary, wash.

Then there were high wires – an extreme version of Go Ape – which were about courage. Some people's lack of suitability for airborne regiments became evident with their legs shaking uncontrollably and genuine terror filling their eyes as they edged one trembling toe in front of the other. There was Combat PT, usually some form of wrestling or hand-to-hand combat, which provided insightful moments; while fear appeared in some people's eyes, a merciless commitment to victory animated others. Plank-offs were another primal and unpleasant challenge. Quite simply, you formed two lines opposite each other, adopted the plank position and held it until you dropped. It became a battle of mind more than body as, almost like dominos, people collapsed until only one remained. All these tests were revealing.

The two culminations of the PT schedule were the 'March and Shoot' and the 'Log Race'. The first was a challenging event involving moving as a platoon with full kit (rifles, bergens etc.) before getting to the range and trying to shoot straight. It was a form of biathlon without the skis, snow or lycra. The results were based on a combination of running time and shooting accuracy. As 41 Platoon didn't want to mess up the apple cart, we continued our rich underperforming vein of form by winning the wooden spoon.

The Log Race was a different story and one that involved zero military competence. In the weeks before, we had several unpleasant training sessions to get us in appropriate shape. Our hands were blistered and our minds resentful. The race was another simple concept: as a platoon, you picked up a log and ran with it as fast as you could around the course, while other platoons did the same. The log itself is *really* heavy. For ten months, we'd each had a rope with a toggle at the end that had remained unused in our bottom drawers but now their true grim purpose was finally revealed as toggle ropes wrapped around the log were the carrying mechanism. Four people lined up either side; the remainder of the platoon ran alongside and did intermittent moving changeovers.

In the days beforehand, platoons eyeing up the top prize suffered mysteriously 'unfortunate' injuries and illnesses which, oddly, took out only their slowest and weakest members. It spoke volumes for their platoon ethos and togetherness. Despite the mathematical impossibility of finishing anything other than last place in the inter-platoon competition, or perhaps because of it, 41 Platoon went to the start line together. We lined up with a combination of abilities, goals and motivations, but we were still the same varied bunch who had trained together since the beginning.

With seven logs for seven platoons laid down in front of us, dread and excitement came over every cadet in CC133. It was yet another rite of passage to add to the back catalogue of others. Eight of us stood with our hands around the ropes and waited to lift our log. The ensuing 3.2 miles would be horrible from the moment the canon fired. It wouldn't get easier by the mile, the pain wouldn't stop, the discomfort wouldn't cease because you wished it. In fact, every mile would be harder, heavier and more demanding of resilience. But every mile would also be one less to go, one closer to the finish.

Off went the canon, up came the log and the mad rush began. Within seconds of moving, colour sergeants and mild-mannered captains were running alongside us shouting anything and everything. They were all those infamous Army terms: gipping, gopping, heaving and hoofing. We were grizzing it but also hanging out. Colour Sergeant Campbell shouted that we could sleep when we were dead, this was the time to work. Colour O'Sullivan bellowed at his platoon, 'EARN YOUR WEEKEND, GENTS, EARN YOUR FUCKING WEEKEND!' The pain was there in my hand as it gripped the frayed old rope. It was in my left forearm as it cried out for relief, my left shoulder as it dipped down to the height of others and my back as it twisted out of shape. All the while, the lactic acid built in my quads and calves as we hauled this bloody thing forwards.

Then we raised our right hands and the next team of eight took over the rope. They drove the log forwards and their pain began. It was so specific and so all-encompassing. For a matter of seconds, minutes at max, we were given a break. As the log continued, we switched sides and ran alongside it. The hands of the carriers then went up, we lined up behind them, took over and drove it forwards, once more providing regular small surges of energy.

We started slowly but our aim was to gradually catch up. We overtook a few teams at the one-mile point, another team after one and a half miles and yet another at the two-mile point. Against expectations, with a little more than a mile to go, we found ourselves in third place. Our changeovers were slick but became less structured as people's energy levels waned. Every time you took the log, you'd be ready to do your bit; but as soon as that weight began to drag, you'd want to raise your hand immediately. The pain was inescapable. The only way out was to stay off the log but that meant someone else going through the suffering. You could see the grimacing, gurning and discomfort on people's faces. There was no 'flow state' or 'runner's high'.

Ascending the final incline, we edged towards O'Sullivan's 40 Platoon. Our front pair roared us forwards. Half the platoon was struggling to just run alongside the log, let alone carry it. O'Sullivan was shouting, 'EARN YOUR FUCKING PAY! MOVE!' but it wasn't enough. Like Oxbridge rowing boats competing for the same bit of water, the two teams fought for the same space but we fought harder. Into second place. A gradual downhill stretch awaited followed by the final push towards the finish line outside Old College. We could see the team from 36 Platoon up ahead, struggling and making errors. This was our chance at the record books. The final right-hand corner awaited. We took the inside line and snuck into the lead. Our opponents were beaten, mentally shot after having been pipped so close to the end. The rank outsiders would win: Buster Douglas beating Mike Tyson in 1990, Goran Ivanisevic at Wimbledon in 2001, Greece at the Euros in 2004, 41 Platoon in the Sandhurst Log Race. It was scripted. Except that the Army gods looking down on our ungainly bodies clearly had a different vision.

The finish line was a matter of metres away. Finally the pain would end. We could collapse, breathe, recover, celebrate. One more surge. 'GOOOO!!!' And then it happened. Eeyore's right bootlace came undone. He was the second man on the left-hand side. He stumbled and lost control of the toggle. He stumbled again and fell backwards into Philipps who in turn stumbled and fell backwards into Russell. All three people were on the ground desperately trying to claw their way up. The other side were hopelessly dragging the log but it wasn't enough. Just as in the film *Cool Runnings,* when Derice looks up as his opponents are celebrating their success in the 100-metre Jamaican Olympic trials, that was us in front of Old College. The pre-race favourites took advantage and crossed the line as we inelegantly picked ourselves up. The Charge of the Light Brigade, Tim Henman or Colin Montgomerie never winning tennis or golf majors, Jonny Brownlee being hauled over the finish line by his brother... and 41 Platoon who had successfully snatched defeat from the jaws of victory.

Bavaria in summer gets seriously hot. But unlike the post-Sandhurst Seychelles beach holidays we dreamed of, we were in a FOB on a training area, unsuccessfully fighting prickly heat and sunstroke for two weeks. Colour Sergeant Campbell reminded us that getting sunburnt was a chargeable offence as a self-inflicted and preventable injury. This was Exercise DYNAMIC VICTORY – our final Sandhurst exercise.

DYNAMIC VICTORY was the culmination of our training. Previous exercises had focused on specific military skills: conventional offensive and defensive operations, hybrid warfare, urban warfare, CBRN training, asymmetric threats and riot control. There were also those, such as LONG REACH, aiming to test our teamwork, organisation, navigational skills and physical robustness. Each one had clear objectives and a clear purpose. In Bavaria, we faced two weeks of complex immersive training in tough conditions. It was also an exercise which Sandhurst threw resources at to create scenarios that felt genuine and insightful. There were bustling local markets with actors playing different roles, something built up through personnel intelligence analysis alongside thorough after-action reviews dissecting our decision-making and situational analysis.

We were kitted out with Tactical Effects Simulation (TESEX) gear, and Big Brother-type GPS trackers of our movement. The 'It wasn't me, Colour Sergeant' line was tough to pull off when a GPS tracker showed who shot what, when and where.

For many, this would be the last time their belt buckle would ever need to touch the ground again. No more leopard-crawling, tactical-bounding, grenade-throwing, hand-signalling or bayoneting. No more moving firing positions after every few shots, wearing cam cream, conducting recce patrols or closing with and killing the enemy. For them, the world of desks, spreadsheets, vehicle moves, intelligence gathering and teaching lay ahead and they were happier for it.

There is a battle-planning rule for officers: one-third, two-thirds. Essentially, you allocate yourself one-third of the time and allow two-thirds to those under your command. This means that if an officer cadet is given an H-hour in 24 hours, they have to conduct a Combat Estimate and come up with three COAs before writing and delivering their orders within eight hours. This then gives their soldiers 16 hours to wash, rest in their green gas chambers, prepare their kit and then move in preparation to leave the harbour area and cross the line of departure.

The process to get there is a bit messier. The inexperienced officer cadet plays internal hurry up and wait while painfully aware of the 'Serve to Lead' ideal before issuing a Warning Order (WngO) – a preliminary notice of an order with essential tasks and timings – without really knowing where they're going, what they're doing and when they need to do it. This is flapping. So he takes a condor moment and locates the black lumi pen he borrowed from someone else the day before. He assesses the missions, tasks and the intent of the company commander (his 1-Up), the New College commander (his 2-Up) and sometimes even his 3-Up, but nobody knows who the hell that is. He analyses his own strengths and weaknesses versus the enemy's. He pores over maps under torchlight as he plans and scribbles as fast as his mind can think. He focuses on the code words, risks, radio signals, contingencies, actions on ambushes, injuries or getting lost. He plans the route in, the timings, the potential entry points, locations and routines of enemy sentry positions.

He likely keeps planning but before he's even got to question three of the fabled Seven Questions, he's set on COA1: a water-tight battle-winning formula. He's got a vague COA2 if asked and an even more vague COA3. He knows he must have a COA3; Sandhurst, the DS and the Seven Questions demand it. If asked, he simply can't not have a COA3. As such, for a Sandhurst cadet under severe time pressure, COA3 is usually very bold and very simple – back-of-a-cigarette-packet-type stuff. COA3 is like the final answer of an exam paper when you've totally misjudged the time allocated but must put something down on paper to avoid getting zero. It's *Rambo* meets *Apocalypse Now.* There are helicopters flying overhead, bombs going off, machine-gun rounds accompanied by a Richard Wagner score and multiple 'battle-winning assets' being utilised. Where it fails in hearts and minds, it wins in simplicity and power. As ever, he wishes he had more time.

To deliver orders, you need a model to show where you are, where you're going and who or what is nearby. The platoon commander is too busy flapping so delegates to a responsible colleague. His aim is to create a physical representation of the ground being covered during the ensuing task. He analyses the map and visualises what he sees on the paper – undulations, rivers, roads, paths and trees – before somehow representing that in a scale model on the empty ground in front of him. He orchestrates others to repurpose soil, leaves, moss, stones, wood, talcum powder, cardboard ammunition boxes and other miscellaneous items to create a nature-inspired 3D version of the map that everyone can see and understand. It's a very simple version of a landscape designer putting their sketches into reality.

Once the model is made, it's time for orders. In a courtroom context, this is a barrister presenting his case to the jury: a performance to demonstrate presenting prowess, poise, personality and passion. The platoon commander stands up with a long wooden pointing stick in one hand and his Tactical Aide Memoire in the other. Everyone else is sitting in a hollow square around the model with cam cream, helmets on and a rifle nearby. He begins in earnest by reminding everyone – in case we weren't aware – what he and they should be doing. He starts with, 'Listen in to a set of orders.'

He begins by identifying the boundaries of the model... to those who created it. The majority of orders cover essential knowledge about timings, logistics and plans for the ensuing actions. We hastily write down notes, preparing for a post-orders cross-examination. At irregular intervals, he tells the heavy-eyed audience to stand up and shake themselves off, and asks a few 'confirmatory questions'. On several occasions he confuses himself by pointing at various objects on the model and referring to them as on his left and our right. He then realises he's flanked and corrects himself, saying they're on his right and our left. Similarly conflicting remarks are made about roads going from west to east, or east to west.

We're then told to put our notebooks down so he can deliver a rousing and impassioned summary. This is a barrister's closing statement. Instructors say that 'a shit set of orders can be saved by a good summary.' I assure you, they can't. Some orders succeed only in sowing confusion rather than providing clarification. A shit set of orders is a shit set of orders. We then conduct a 'watch sync': 30 people waiting with their fingers poised ready to click the reset button on their Combat Casio. With watches synced, orders are over. The platoon commander's one-third is over. 'You're in your own time now.' It's time to settle our heads deep into our green hot dogs before we head off for the beginning of the end.

⌐— ⌐

The two weeks in Bavaria went by with the expected peaks and troughs, but at a more realistic tempo than other exercises which had been full throttle with zero downtime. The one-third/two-thirds rule was generally adhered to and we were given more time to think and plan before acting effectively. Most of us were conscientious and didn't want to mess others around with excessive hurry up and waits. But Field Marshal Slim's 'just plain you' was also a hazardous blank canvas for those on the cusp of commissioning.

For the Commodore, DYNAMIC VICTORY was quite the opportunity. Impressively, astoundingly, until the final attack, he managed to not fire a single shot. Sleep when you're dead didn't work for him; sleep when you're in Bavaria was preferable. Boots-off gonkers was very much a thing and each time the Commodore whipped out his green fruit roll-up, he claimed it exemplified his 'fight smart, not hard' methodology. As we sometimes lay awake in full kit, we wondered if perhaps the Commodore was winning after all.

The exercise culminated in one final attack.

This wasn't a section, platoon or company-level assault. It was a battalion one. The command appointments were at a higher level and the top cadet from Falklands and Imjin respectively oversaw their company. All the stops were pulled out. We utilised helicopters to increase the speed and scope of our plan, there was artillery – real and simulated – to show the traditional dynamics of an assault, where the heavy shelling served to break the cohesion and will of the enemy before ground troops moved in. Enemy tanks patrolled the objective and we had to systematically coordinate our tactics to eliminate those battle-winning assets. Upon commissioning, we would head in our separate directions – diving, bomb disposal, air assault, mechanical engineering, reconnaissance – but, in that moment, regardless of our future cap badges, we were all soldiers waiting at the line of departure for our synchronised watches to work in a harmonious dream. We had done the planning, coordinated timings, codewords, passwords, boundaries, contingencies and deconflictions.

At H minus 1 – one minute before H-hour – two platoons from Imjin Company unloaded their magazines with a volley of fire support. The seconds ticked by. At 05:59:50, 'CHECK FIRE!' was called and the fire support stopped. Ten seconds of silence. The digital numbers flicked from 05:59:59 to 06:00:00. A tap on the shoulder of the lead man and our assault began. Moving from the south and going clockwise, 41 Platoon headed out. Other platoons were coming from the north.

It sounds a bit dramatic saying we stormed the buildings. We and the enemy had blank rounds, and although they were not quite as compliant as our favourite enemy from Gurkha

Company Sittang, it still felt like high-quality match-fixing. Regardless, we efficiently proceeded from one house to the next, enacting the plan our commanders had put in place. In Inters, Colour Sergeant Campbell had told me that when I began to take the exercises seriously, as though the enemy was real, I would extract more from them. If you treat it like training, like it doesn't matter, like you can take shortcuts and take the easy option, then what do you expect in the real heat of battle? For those who would never do it again, they wanted to do it properly and leave on a high knowing they had given their best. We all did. Our professionalism at an individual and collective level was higher than it ever had been.

After neutralising the enemy threats and clearing all the key buildings, we stood near the windows of the houses we had occupied, keeping watch and waiting. Some remained attentive, having been caught unprepared on previous occasions. Others sat, smoked a cigarette and took a moment to acknowledge this satisfying moment in the Bavarian hills. And then we heard it: 'STOOOOPPPPPPPP!' We all joined in the elongated use of the single word, knowing it signalled the end.

The whole intake, all members of CC133 including our instructors, were then called together and stood in a hollow square. The commandant stood before us and said a few words about the journey we'd gone on through training, praising our professionalism on the exercise and encouraging us to be proud and humble.

We were then told to remove our Sandhurst berets, the one that had been rained on and sweated in since the beginning. We each replaced it with the beret of the regiment we would subsequently join. Infanteers had their brown berets, the Parachute Regiment maroon, Army Air Corps sky blue, Royal Military Police red, Intelligence Corps cypress green, cavalry blue. Scots had their

Tam o'Shanter while the Royal Irish a caubeen. Those new berets were not gifted or presented; they had been earned through time, effort and determination. It was a symbolic moment, one to recognise our journey and a glimpse into the future.

Colour Sergeant Campbell then spoke to the platoon.

'Gents, that was… satisfactory.' He smiled. It was the best we were going to get. 'Now, brass picking. Get to it, ya mutants!'

Chapter 10

Officer Cadet Lombard, 41 Platoon, was delighted. In just two weeks' time, he would banish the rank of officer cadet forever, earn his commission, and become a second lieutenant; the commissioning course was on the cusp of completion. Lombard and the other future cavalry officers of CC133 were given a call to arms by their prospective regiments and made their way to one of the many Sandhurst function rooms for a brief. No uniform was to be worn; it was chinos, shirts, ties and tweed jackets.

A few high-ranking officers gave brief briefs about their time at Sandhurst and life as a junior officer. They were rose-tinted anecdotes but with positive sentiments. The sergeant major present, Jenkins, a man we'd never seen before, scanned the room. His eyes darted from cadet to cadet as we avoided his glare. His leathery face was in a state of permafrown.

A few were note-taking. Maybe something to refer back to, to look busy or because the habit was force-fed into the Sandhurst water supply. Lombard was a charming top-of-the-middle-third cadet, with a propensity towards heavy boozing and an enviable natural fitness. He was a blue-sky big thinker prone to glossing over the nitty-gritty detail. Lombard did not have his waterproof notebook and black pen to hand. After the brigadier had recounted another dit, Sergeant Major Leatherface called a halt to proceedings and requested that all 15 people present hold up their notebooks and pens. Lombard held his iPhone aloft.

'What's that?'

'It's my iPhone, sir.'

'Why is your iPhone here?'

'To take notes, sir.'

'Future regiment?'

'King's Royal Hussars, sir.'

'I was the RSM of that regiment.' RSM, regimental sergeant major, is the top-ranking soldier in a regiment. Junior officers are recommended to steer well clear of them for their own safety and sanity. 'Tell me what's wrong with a notebook and pen, Mr Lombard?'

'Nothing, sir.'

'Well, why is your phone in your hand then, Mr Lombard?'

All others present shuffled our feet in uneasy anticipation. Most knew better than to attract the attention of Sergeant Major Leatherface. All except Officer Cadet Lombard who refused to accept his unwinnable position.

'Well, sir…'

What followed this 'Well, sir…' could never go down well.

Lombard continued. 'With my phone I can type down what's being said, edit it, save it and share it. In addition, my phone is always accessible so I can refer to the brigadier's notes on leadership whenever I feel I need direction.'

It was a classy touch. In one fell swoop, we'd switched loyalties to the unprepared, sycophantic, arse-kissing iPhone note-taker.

Leatherface was the kind of man to pull out the 'I was doing Special Ops while you were eating Coco Pops' line whenever he was on the back foot. Instead, he went with, 'Look, Mr Lombard, I was in Baghdad while you were in your dad's bag. Everyone else has a notebook and pen except you. Hasn't Sandhurst taught you anything?'

Conformity and convention were classic arguments that the old regularly levelled at the new, the 'Why change something that works?' or 'We've always done it this way' mentality. Lombard had an opportunity. A young pretender meets an old master: Darth Vader versus Obi-Wan Kenobi, Federer versus Sampras at Wimbledon, an officer cadet versus a sergeant major at Sandhurst. This revolutionary was not going down without a fight.

Leatherface wasn't finished. 'Not that you'd know but you won't have a phone with you on operations.'

'Perhaps not, sir, but I'm not sure I'll have my Sandhurst notepad either.'

Battle-weary Leatherface needed a comeback of Lazarus-esque proportions.

'But... what if your phone runs out of battery?'

'What if my pen runs out of ink, sir?'

'And... and what if you lose your phone?'

With that question, it was over. Lombard let the question hang in the air, its feebleness not even deserving a response.

The conversation moved on. This battle of background, age, experience, foresight and indoctrination would continue another day.

⌘ — ⌘

Our wall charts were now like an Advent calendar in the days leading up to Christmas, with only a few remaining.

We had our final chapel service. The services at Sandhurst are traditional, what's known as 'muscular Christianity' – the belief in patriotic duty, self-sacrifice and discipline is reflected in rousing hymns such as 'I Vow to Thee, my Country', 'Jerusalem' and the national anthem. All were undeniably impactful in that setting with everyone in their smartest military uniforms knowing it would be their final appearance in that iconic building. The feeling of being there, surrounded by the names on the walls of officers who had once stood in our places and who had paid the ultimate sacrifice, made the hairs on the back of your neck come to life, made you stand that bit taller, that bit straighter, and sing with more heart.

Those fateful words, '*Dulce et decorum est pro patria mori*', written above our heads by the doors. Thoughts about our training, the war graves, bayonets, machine guns, snipers, pistols and grenades permeated once more. There were questions, too, the same questions we had discussed so many times before, about our future roles and the values we stood for.

We were fitted by tailors for our future regimental mess dress and had our final formal dinner. The grey men and women of CC133 were pleased to be the ones on the edge of Michelangelo's *Last Supper*, away from the prying eyes and ears of the most senior-ranking officials present. Gone were the heady days of Junior term where gaining a central spot was an ambition rather than a burden.

We also conducted our final interviews with our platoon commanders, in my case with Captain Connolly.

In most lines of work, a simple knock or gentle peek around the door usually suffices. Alas, not in the Army. 'The Army is a vocation, a lifestyle, not a job, Mr Stewart' is what I am constantly told. As such, I march up to the door, come to attention with my hands rigid by my sides and salute. At this point, with my right thumb above my right eye and my palm facing outwards, I wait. I hope that Captain Connolly has noticed me. He hasn't. Instead, he's gesticulating wildly at his computer for being 'in clip'. His old MGB car is often berated for being 'in clip'. The platoon's 'terrorist bottom-third' are consistently 'in clip'. Through his profession-alism and quirks, the captain has become someone we are intrigued by, and fond of, in equal measure. Captain Connolly thrives in the Army. He loves soldiering and the rigidity of Sandhurst.

I'm there outside the door and mid-salute. I gently cough to get his attention.

'Sir, may I have your leave to fall in, sir, please.' Even now, in week 44, we go through the process of asking permission to enter someone's room using this precise phraseology.

'Good morning, Mr Stewart, take a seat.' I sit. 'Mr Stewart, this computer... it's fucking embarrassing.' He, like so many in the Army, has a go-to swear word to break up sentences. We speak about my performance at Sandhurst over the year before discussing my longer-term plans. I give typically down-the-line responses about serving my soldiers and seeing what happened after.

'Just make sure you're not one of those thousand-day types. They... they make my blood boil, Mr Stewart. Take the good bits and don't give back. It's fucking shit.'

Thousand-day soldiers are those that serve the minimum amount of time – around three years post-Sandhurst – before leaving the Army. That sort of attitude is inconsistent with Captain Connolly's unwavering concept of performing your duty regardless of the sacrifices and service involved.

We speak about other aspects of the course, my choice of regiment and the quirks in the way Sandhurst operates. We shake hands.

I repeat those absurd lines once more: 'Sir, may I have your leave to fall out, sir, please.'

'Please do, Mr Stewart.'

I salute, do an about-turn and march away from his office for the final time.

⌒ — ⌒

'What are you so scared of? It's just hay that's been eaten!'

It was one of the final parade practices before the big day. The Bear was on the prowl watching our every move like an oversized, barrel-chested, bicep-popping hawk. Patel, Lombard and I – the three tallest members of the platoon – were at the front in boots and combats, marching not just the platoon but the whole intake onto the parade square. As per our training, there was a skill in foreseeing dangers and spotting the presence of the abnormal. The abnormal here was a large mound of horse turd positioned about fifty metres in front of our current position. On our current trajectory, at our current pace, we'd connect in approximately forty-five seconds. The combined knowledge of billions of humans over hundreds of thousands of years had taught us that the sole of a shoe and shit should never interact.

The Bear, also a *Homo sapien* despite the name, was aware of this. He, too, had spent his life avoiding walking in shit. He stalked just ahead of us. The 45 seconds quickly became 30 then 20. Nobody had said a word but we were cognisant of the danger.

The Bear was also aware. 'Keep your course, gentlemen.'

I was front left. I whispered to Lombard, 'Not happening, mate.' Despite the Bear's instructions, we'd drifted slightly left. I was currently safe, Patel was in the firing line, Lombard on the cusp. With expert control and before I had time to correct the situation, Patel edged right and the platoon followed. Ten seconds left. I had no choice but to follow. He was now safe, but I was in trouble. Lombard remained on the cusp.

The Bear saw this all unfold, which inspired his 'It's just hay that's been eaten' line. I veered away at the final moment. The person behind me, Travers, managed to make a final swerve as well, like a cyclist seeing a pothole at the last second. After that, all we heard was squelching feet and a long series of cussing. The Commodore, it transpired, had placed his size 10s plonk in the middle. We grinned.

The parade finished. It had been lacklustre, the sort of performance reminiscent of aged TV stars coming back for a money-spinning reunion: unmemorable, been better and lacking spark. Immediately following the parade, alongside most of the permanent staff, all six hundred or so Sandhurst cadets arranged themselves in a hollow square outside New College for skits.

Skits are a key part of Army life: a comedy sketch, almost always a parody, public piss-taking performed by soldiers. Given its purpose, the Army can take itself quite seriously, but skits are a great diffuser. They're usually a chance for light-hearted friendly fire at your bosses targeting their quirks, mannerisms and failings, performed in good humour and with good intentions and received in the same vein.

Throughout the intake, we had worked on impersonations and zeroed in on the mannerisms, tics and language exhibited by the Sandhurst personalities. Spend that much intensive time with anyone, especially in such a surreal setting, and you struggled to hide much.

During our final exercise in Bavaria, a few of us were doing impersonations, knowing our skits were a few weeks' away. Gradually, our idea came to fruition. The concept was simple: a game of *The Weakest Link* with the host, Anne Robinson, played by me aiming to represent our company commander, Major Stevens. The contestants were other members of the Academy played by members of Falklands Company dressed as we wanted to convey them, likely not always consistent with how they wanted to be portrayed. Few people escaped the firing line, ranging from the commandant and sergeant majors down to the PT staff, range staff and armourers. Sod the ambushes, raids and recces; this was *the* serious command appointment – the culmination of my leadership training. Our 15-minute sketch was a compilation of in-jokes, personal jibes, direct quotations, stereotyping and light-hearted criticisms. We collectively adopted the 'Seek forgiveness, not permission' mentality.

The next day is a Wednesday morning in early August; we're due to commission on Friday. We're in blues, an immediate performance-raiser as the realism of what we're doing becomes more evident. Our progression is hard to halt now. Before we make the move to the Old College parade square, we line up as an intake with a few minutes to kill. For instructors, dead time for Sandhurst cadets is time that should be filled. As such, a particularly passionate sergeant major from the Irish Guards, whom we've never encountered before, decides to give us some of what he calls 'remedial rifle drill'. In sync, every officer cadet follows the commands he shrieks in a remarkably high-pitched voice. He's less than enamoured with our attempts.

'You're allowed to strike the weapon. Don't let me stop you. Don't hold back. Go for it.' His sarcasm and frustration are evident. This movement in rifle drill involved slapping your right hand flush against the harsh metal of your SA80 rifle. Few, if any, do this move with enthusiasm. It's uncomfortable and makes your white gloves less white, a punishable error. We pat the rifle instead. 'Gents, start switching on or we'll have to warm up again.'

It transpires that he prefers his striking to our patting, so we 'warm up' again. This entails a hitherto unknown method of torture whereby we hold the five-kilogram rifle outwards parallel to the floor. We then hold it upwards and out to the side at right angles. We then make circles of increasing size with the tips of our bayonets. He then issues the simple line, 'I hope we all now remember to STRIKE!… SEIZE!… and GRASP! the weapon.' And then, just like that, the volatile Irish sergeant major marches off never to be seen again. He has only ever been spoken about in nervous undertones since that ten-minute cameo, but his memory most certainly lives on. 'STRIKE!... SEIZE!... and GRASP! the weapon.' Six words that we'll never forget.

We begin to march on for this final practice, the dress rehearsal: the Commandant's Parade. Patel, Lombard and I are grateful for the now turdless parade ground. For the first time, a band is accompanying us. It suddenly feels very... real, as though all the practice, all the tweaking, the sparking and switching on has come to something. Given it's the final practice, the standards are impeccably high and the Bear is stalking the company once again.

He's warned us that 'Any mistakes today and I'll be all over you like a cheap suit.' It's either that or being all over us 'like a rash' or, even more colourfully, 'like a tramp on chips'. Thankfully, I avoid the first wave of attacks. First off, it's Mardirossoyan who is told to 'Stop catching flies' following his open-mouthed confusion. The mistake isn't remedied so the Bear follows up saying, 'Shut your mouth, Mr Mardirossoyan, you're like a Venus flytrap.' Others on parade are described as being 'about as much use as a chocolate fireguard' and having 'The wisdom of youth and the energy of old age'.

As we stand there, rifles in hand, eyes focused dead ahead and trying not to move, the Bear wanders over.

'How are your arms, Mr Stewart?'

'Not bad thanks, Sergeant Major. How are yours?'

'Massive, as always.'

On a left wheel before the walk past, the Academy sergeant major happens to be lurking. This is a man who once described himself as 'like Sauron, the all-seeing eye'. A few weeks before, he had caught a member of 37 Platoon leaving the Academy grounds in a pair of jeans. The cadet in question, Mr Haston, was informed, 'Denim is the devil's cloth, Mr Haston. Only civilians wear denim. And civilians have bad habits like taking drugs, walking slowly and giving up.' Back to the left wheel.

'Oi, you, Anne Robinson!'

His gaze is aimed directly at me. *Oh shit*. He's an intimidating man but amusing when he wants to be – his tendency to refer to any shorter member of the intake as 'Bilbo', 'Frodo' or 'Baggins' is a popular line of attack. He's the most senior non-commissioned soldier at Sandhurst and I am now in his crosshairs. He was also, I recall, one of our losing Weakest Link contestants.

'Who, me, sir?

'Who? Don't *who me*. I'm not a fucking owl.'

'Roger, sir.'

'Sir?! I'm not a fucking officer. Only God calls me sir and he does that because I'm in charge here.' He pauses. 'Anne Robinson, that was one of the best skits I've seen in the Army. Now… suck in your piss tank, neck to the back of your collar, get on the heel and get those arms shoulder-high.'

⌐ — ⌐

The day had come. Our wall charts were now row upon row of days crossed out with an 'X'. When I first saw my wall chart, those exercise names and checkpoints to go through were just that: names on a chart. They meant something different now – each name had its own memories forever associated with it. Every box had been ticked; every square successfully navigated. Except one, the CC133 Commissioning Parade. That was *the* box, the culmination of all the rest. We knew what needed to be done.

The morning flew by with alarms, critical timings, preparation, five minutes before five minutes before, hurrying and waiting and last-minute flapping. We were all paranoid about someone accidentally touching the shimmering toe caps of our boots, having spent painful hours making them glisten. We did our final buddy-buddy check to remove fluff, re-straighten hats and realign jacket buttons. We exited the door to the New College parade square and marched out to form up in our platoons. Each of us knew every inch of the parade square and every word that would be uttered over the ensuing 90 minutes. From the first day at Sandhurst until the last, this was the moment everything built up to, the crescendo of the symphony. And in the distance, on the Old College parade square, was a stand filled with our friends and families. This was the day we'd waited and prepared for, not just since Ironing Board Sunday, but also since that first hungover interview in Dundee all those years before. There was no backing out now; the train was almost at the station and we just needed to stay aboard.

'Gentlemen, you should be proud of what you've achieved. Your families are looking on, excited to see you. But this is *your* day. *You've* earned this moment. *You've* earned the right to be here and to march up those steps. Now go out there and act like you're the smartest men in the world.' That was all the Bear needed to say.

The Academy sergeant major then took centre stage and Sauron's all-seeing eye surveyed those in front of him.

'Commissioning Course 133. Take the atmosphere in. Remember this moment. This is your day. Live the Sandhurst dream. And please look after and lead our men and women with all the dedication and professionalism I know you're capable of.'

And then the symbols crashed and the band started.

'By the right, quick... MARCH!'

Our footsteps were aligned perfectly to the sound of the drumbeat and each other. Chins up, heads back, arms shoulder-high. There was purpose in our synchronisation. Butterflies were present as we marched forwards, step by step onto the same parade square we had been up and down so many times before. The band played 'Soldiers of the Queen'. The crowd was silent.

The band stopped. The only noise was the feet of the Senior term cadets. We found our mark, remained in line and waited for the words of command.

'SANDHURST!' We knew what was coming. It had to be good. First impressions counted. As Colour Sergeant Campbell always said, 'Perception is king.'

'SANDHUUUUURST... SHUN!'

The raw sound of hard-soled drill boots crashing into the concrete below echoed through the silence.

'LEEEEFFFFT... TURN!'

All those one-liners fed to us by our instructors came down to these moments. In one sudden move, our bodies lurched to the left and we grew in the turn. 'STAND STILL!' and 'SHUT YOUR MOUTHS!' we had been told again and again. There was no need on this occasion. We all stood proud and motionless.

Each of us caught a glimpse of our families in the stands. Their eyes were scanning the front row, trying to spot their sons or daughters. As much as we all wanted to wink, smile and get their attention, that could wait. For this brief period, we needed to maintain our professionalism, as if to prove what we had learned by not becoming distracted. We marched around the parade square in quick and slow time. We presented arms to the Queen. We were inspected by the Chief of the General Staff. Somehow, we remained in step and in time throughout. Who were we performing for? Those watching, yes. Ourselves and our instructors, of course. It was also for those to the left and right of us. Those people we had laughed, learned and moaned with. This was our parade. We all wanted to get it right, to not let the side down, to not be the broken link in the chain.

The Academy adjutant, sitting atop his white mare, then gave another command.

'The Senior Division... inward... TURN!' The Junior and Intermediate cadets remained facing forwards. We turned inwards to face the centre of the parade square.

The Academy adjutant shouted once more.

'The remainder... PRESEEEEENT ARMS!'

'The Senior Division... inwards wheel, by the centre... slooooow MARCH!'

The drumbeat sounded once more as the band played 'Auld Lang Syne'. The 190 officer cadets from Commissioning Course 133 slow-marched, conducted a right turn and then headed towards the steps of Old College; the same steps I had first walked up in my suit with an ironing board under my arm 44 weeks earlier. This time, with a rifle in my left hand, it felt rather different. We went up, two by two. One footstep for each drumbeat on each of the steps, between those faded white pillars and into the foyer.

No mistakes, not this time. When it mattered most, we all performed.

We then handed in our rifles and walked, yes walked, not marched, onto the parade square to see our families. I've seen pride in my parents' eyes before but not like this. The tears in my mum's eyes said more than the words she spoke.

Almost all our training had been done in this secretive world behind barbed wire fences inside the Sandhurst bubble. We shared anecdotes and showed photos to our friends and family. They commented on our new language and new haircuts but, for the vast majority, Sandhurst was a world away from anything they could make sense of. Up until the day I had entered the gates with my mum and girlfriend, it was a world I could barely have made sense of. But that moment, when I walked towards my waiting family with glistening boots, polished buttons and pressed uniform, it felt as though it did somehow make sense and as though the effort had been worth it.

⌒ — ⌒

That evening, we replaced our blues with our regimental mess dress as we prepared for the Commissioning Ball. My parents, uncles and aunts were replaced by friends, as we transitioned from the parade square to the party. The music played, shocking dance moves were performed and drinks were consumed with zeal. Yes, we were still in uniform and, yes, we were still on Sandhurst grounds, but it was a chance to let our hair down, pull the pin and genuinely celebrate.

Until midnight, as per Sandhurst tradition, each of us kept the rank slides on our shoulders concealed. Until midnight, we were officer cadets in training. At midnight, however, the fireworks were set off, the fabric over our rank slides was removed and the solitary pip representing the rank of second lieutenant was visible. With that, we officially became commissioned officers in the British Army.

The night continued at pace. Champagne was drunk and the sodden dancefloor collected stumbling guests, while the male and female platoons took the opportunity to become acquainted with each other – as confirmed by the sheepish re-emergence of various new male officers from the female lines the next morning.

At 0700, the horrendous sound of a fire alarm pierced through our throbbing skulls. I resignedly stood outside my room along-side a selection of other ropey-looking officers. For the most part, we had all managed to stumble and stagger our way to the right place at the right time. A hangover and a hazy complexion were part of the anticipated fallout from the chaos of the night before.

Sandhurst was not quite finished with us. We shovelled down breakfast as best as possible, filled out a few forms, returned kit and filled out a few more forms. In about the most unglamorous and insignificant way, we were presented with our scrolls – a complicated and barely legible bit of text from the Queen reminding us of our new job role and her endorsement of it. None of our heads were quite mindful enough to appreciate the moment. And then there was the clear up.

The saying goes that you should never return to the scene of a crime. Return to the marquee and sports field we did, though, and were immediately ordered around by the same instructors, in the same place, and with the same results. The only thing that had changed were three small letters. Out of custom and professionalism, regardless of their sentiments, each colour sergeant added 'sir' at the end of their request. Despite this novel formality, those in charge were certainly not among the 190 junior officers on their hands and knees picking up cigarette butts and broken glass and whinging about their hangovers.

Nobody quite knows why Sandhurst puts its new officers through this little ritual but three potential reasons stand out. First, most of us had to drive home and were far over the limit. Second, given the job had to be done by someone, why not save the cleaning costs and utilise the skilled labour available – it's not like we were going to be given a lie-in. Third, and most importantly, was humility. Becoming an officer was evidently, and rightfully, a source of pride for us all. None of us could have made it through the course without the support of our colour sergeants. A few things change as the clock strikes midnight, but most don't.

Sandhurst's motto is 'Serve to Lead'. As a second lieutenant, you're the lowest officer rank in the British Army and you're certainly not too grand to do the lowest jobs. Lombard told me that getting our commission felt something like chasing the end of a rainbow; searching and searching for something then realising the situation was unchanged and we were still without a pot of gold. Picking up cigarette butts reminds you of your place in the circle of Army life.

Finally, as the alcohol levels dropped and the dehydration started to kick in, we were given the green light to depart. I said goodbye to those I had gone through training with from our first morning on the line to standing side by side on the parade square. I then sought out Colour Sergeant Campbell. Sandhurst is unique in placing such training responsibility on senior non-commissioned soldiers, our platoon colour sergeants. Colour Sergeant Campbell and I had built a relationship of mutual understanding, respect and fondness. Of course, since we were both in the Army, British and male, our brief parting conversation spoke volumes.

'Colour Sergeant, thank you and farewell. It's been a pleasure.'

'The pleasure, sir, has been all mine. Keep in touch, Mr Stewart, and good luck.'

I put my final belongings in an Army-issue cardboard box and squeezed it into the boot of my car alongside a selection of books, boots, camouflage clothing and, of course, an ironing board.

At ten miles per hour, I gently rolled away leaving Old College in my rearview mirror. I handed in my Sandhurst car pass at the exit gate and headed home.

Chapter 11

In Junior term we'd been trained not to think, to follow orders and observe direction: move there, carry this, shoot that. We needed to be soldiers, followers, teammates, disciples. As Intermediate term progressed, we needed to know what to think while remembering how to think: to lead, solve problems, improvise, adapt and overcome. Come Seniors, the reins were loosened again. We had to learn to understand, interpret and analyse. We had to foresee and decipher complexity; outthink and outmanoeuvre the enemy; observe, orient, decide and act. We had to recognise and embrace leadership, responsibility and command. Soon the reins would be removed again with no platoon commander, colour sergeant or CSM lurking over our shoulders coaching us into the right position.

So much and so little had changed in those 44 weeks. It would shape the direction of my life for the ensuing few years at least. In reality, the next few weeks were my only current horizon – the uncertainty of future deployments would likely determine the period ahead. I wondered in the days and weeks after whether Sandhurst had fundamentally changed me rather than simply endowing me with a wealth of knowledge and temporary habits. And, if so, how? How would the classes we sat in, the people we observed, the challenges we faced and the skills we learned impact us? I had asked a friend the same question shortly before he commissioned. He thought and simply said, 'I think it's made me a better person.'

Straight after commissioning, I thought less of it. I thought less of some people I worked alongside given their limitations as soldiers and potential officers. Some of those sentiments remain but your ability to coordinate a fireteam attack in the wind and rain in Brecon is of less importance than your values, empathy, selflessness and resilience. In many ways, the relentless rhythm of Sandhurst does not lend itself to creating quieter, more thoughtful individuals. Those people, who often become highly effective officers, do not get the credit they deserve in that formulaic, tramlined and testosterone-filled environment. Sandhurst, through its constant pursuit of conformity and competitiveness, ignored many of the softer essentials of leadership in favour of immediate and observable ones. Its awards procedure and ranking system benefitted those who played the game and said the right things to the right people instead of those who genuinely looked out for the weaker members of their platoon.

In our penultimate week, we were asked whether anything on the course had been pointless. We were given a few minutes to think before being chosen to answer.

The ideas came thick and fast. Switching rooms in Senior term. Meaningless show parades. Colour coordinating our sock drawer. Making our folded socks smile instead of frown. Learning to march. Needing to march everywhere on camp. Wearing a jacket and tie to enter and exit camp. Wearing the same ill-fitting cotton PT T-shirts as had been done 50 years before. Carrying our Costa coffee cups in a plastic bag or decanting them into a flask. Future teachers and logisticians joining infanteers to conduct platoon attacks on final exercise. Using issue kit instead of better kit. Explaining the boundaries of the model. The excessive daily uniform changes. Having to wear Speedos not swimming trunks. Learning to 'silent swim' thus creating no splashes. Why confirmed cadets were allowed when everyone else went through RSBs. Wearing Army-issue trainers regardless of our foot shape. Why every time kit was issued, the quartermaster said, 'Here you go, one times helmet for the use thereof.' What 'slightly relax' meant and why we were instructed to adopt that position in the lecture theatre. Signing out extra equipment from the store cupboard to make up the weight for a TAB. And, of course, having to sweep leaves in the darkness in the wind in autumn for a VIP visit the following day.

Despite all the suggestions floated, I could not think of one pointless thing. Everything had a direct or indirect purpose, either for the course, for our development or, crucially, for the unique cohesion it created. Every commissioned officer in the British Army, past or present, has gone through Sandhurst and been treated the same way. They have each spent time in that extraordinary environment and got through it. In isolation, that might seem meaningless – perhaps like so many things we had to do. But there's purpose to that meaninglessness. It's almost important because of the shared knowledge that each officer has gone through the same thing.

Ask other officers from other intakes and their list would be equally ridiculous. No officer can forget their platoon colour sergeant. Indeed, what's known as the 'colour sergeant conscience' remains with you long after midnight during your Commissioning Ball. Their sayings, isms and values are the Jiminy Cricket on your shoulder throughout your time as an officer. 'My Men, My Weapon, Myself. I am always in command appointment from the minute I wake.' Or 'You're not there to be friends with your soldiers; you're there to lead.' Or simply 'doing the right thing not the easy thing'. At Sandhurst, the expected standard is set. Whether you choose to adhere to that in future years, or whether you choose to tread over the line, is your very conscious decision.

No officer will ever forget their first day: nervous, excited, unsure. Nor will they forget the moment they slow-marched up the steps of Old College: composed, self-assured, proud. They will remember the final stretch of the 1.5-mile running route along the New College parade square. They will remember the room inspections and the moment they commissioned as officers at midnight surrounded by their friends. The stories, history, quirks, ups, downs, hardship and celebration make Sandhurst the place it is. There is no other military training academy like it and likely never will be. Whether that makes it the best or not, I can't truly say, but it's unique and it sets a high bar. Despite that praise, there's no way I'd want to do it again and I reckon you'd be hard pushed to find another officer who would. And perhaps that too is why Sandhurst is, well, Sandhurst.

'The Army is basically the X-Men for people with no powers and an inability to function in the civilian world', according to one member of CC133, admittedly in hyperbolic fashion. The Army is not like other jobs or organisations. With most types of employment, you do your work, stress, complain, worry about deadlines, work extra hours, help others where possible, lose some free time and take holidays as and when you can. As a government employee, the scrutiny is higher but the principle remains; you do your work and get paid accordingly.

The difference, however, is the end goal of many jobs differs from that of the Army. The Army builds the teamwork, cohesion, stamina, strength, identity and belonging because of what it *could* entail. You could be deployed anywhere and at any time. You could lose your weekends and holidays. You could be sent away for six months and not see your parents, wife or husband.

You could miss the birth of your new child or miss a family Christmas because you were on duty abroad on a deployment you don't quite understand. You could be required to patrol into a city and risk getting shot. You could be required to pick up the person next to you and carry them to safety. Or the person next to you could be required to do the same for you. That's why each one of those nicknames, pranks, nights out, T-shirts and skits matter. It's because, when you really need people to go on a patrol in a foreign country, the people you serve with have chosen to join you.

Only 15 per cent of the Army are officers. Choosing to go to Sandhurst is a very conscious decision. For an officer, there is constant responsibility for the people under your command: 'Serve to Lead'. There are specific skills, knowledge and language one learns in the Army and, if nothing else, I hope this book has given you a little insight into these peculiarities.

The institution, the system, whatever you want to call it, has its obvious flaws – which system doesn't? After you leave, however, those flaws become something you're almost fond of. Making your bed, shining your shoes and getting on and off that bus are parts of it; something you can look beyond and laugh at. But the people, they really matter.

Some people call Sandhurst Hogwarts with guns. Others call it Hogwarts without the magic. Maybe it's a combination of both. There's no magic to Sandhurst but there's still something magical about it. As you drive in, that austere rectangular building has a pull that inspires respect. The commissioning course is a lifelong bond you share with those you went through training alongside; it's not magic, but it's something special.

There was no magic to each of Colour Sergeant Campbell's 'Just confirm'-type questions. I write this now and almost miss his room inspections. *Just one more*, I think, for fun, for the absurdity of it, for the superfluous space between my knife and fork, for people using black permanent pens to cover dirt on their magazines, putting cardboard under their duvets so that they looked rigid, and not using their taps for fear of getting a show parade for having a wet sink. As our knowledge of the system developed, the 'hurry up and wait' mentality became another accepted thing. It was almost embraced.

Rush here, sit there. Get there five minutes before and stand there. No, get there five minutes before five minutes. You're now too early! Complete a fitness test then collapse. Complete a platoon attack then sit in a hollow square. Stop-start, start-stop. Run fast, stand still; run faster, stand stiller; run until you're ill, stand until you fall. Make your bed, clean your rifle, await inspection. March onto the square, stand to attention. One place left. Correction, right. Now halt! Now left again. Now halt! Quick march, slow march. Now Break! Into! Quick! Time! Last in, first out. Shit, no, it's first in, last out. Selfish commitment. Wrong, selfless commitment. If you're not jacking on your soldiers, you're jacking on yourself. That can't be right, it's serve your soldiers. Train easy, fight hard. Fuck, I meant, train hard, fight easy. H-hour is in five minutes. Bollocks, it's H-hour now. ATTACK! You're on leave. No, you're not, you're on duty. All leave is cancelled. Get in your bouncing bomb. Mate, get up, you're on stag. No you're not, you're on the log. It's boots-off gonkers. Get back on the log again. Take risks but not that risk. Fail but don't fail like that. Be yourself but do it in uniform. Delegate but stay in control. Empower but take responsibility. Self-select, don't de-select. On the bus, off the bus. No, everybody back on the bus again. Which bus? The other bus? Right, everyone on the other bus, we should have been there yesterday. Give yourself a show parade!

That was training. It was absurd, hilarious, brilliant, demanding and unforgettable. I hated it and loved it. We all loved to hate it, except for those who genuinely hated or loved it. For most of us, we were somewhere in that large grey area in the middle, purgatory between high-flyers and anchors. We flapped a bit unnecessarily, made mistakes, got immensely fit, lived through it and laughed. And that was that. If I was a more stoic individual, a Major John Majendie type, I could have simply said, 'I suppose we just got on with it' and nothing further would be said. And, in our own ways, we kind of did, because that's just what you do in the Army, you get on with it. Your stress is both justified and pointless. Your goals are both consequential and arbitrary. It's contradiction after contradiction. But that's what training teaches you to do time and time again: you hurry up and wait.

Another officer once said to me he wished he knew how many half-smoked cigarettes were consumed by the Army every day. The half-smoked cigarette is a regular and illustrative occurrence. It is evidence of a changed plan when you've got on the bus and off again. You've waited and waited before finally lighting that cigarette, had a couple of drags and then, it happens, and, sirs, ma'ams, ladies and gents, it happens, right now, shit bust. So, you roll your eyes, you drop your half-smoked cigarette, squash it under the tread of your boots, put your beret back on – obviously, you can't smoke with your beret on – and hurry up doing whatever it is you're meant to be doing. That is until you aren't doing it anymore, whereupon you're waiting. It's confirmation you've just lost another game of Army.

Acknowledgements

Writing and publishing a book, like many military endeavours, is a truly collaborative process requiring selflessness, diligence and trust. Though recognition is no doubt the last thing on their minds, there are many people I need to thank.

First of all, the soldiers I had the privilege to work with, serve under and lead, to whom I have dedicated this book. Since handing in my Army ID, I've had time to better understand the unique bond that exists between those who serve. Fundamentally it's you who inspired me to put pen to paper.

Thanks to D Company for your unrivalled resourcefulness in dodging command appointments and unwavering commitment to the pursuit of mediocrity. Both our approach and the humour that informed it originated in the very early days at Sandhurst and continues to the present. This book couldn't have happened without you.

In a similar vein, recognition is due to those in Imjin Company, CC133. We of Falklands Company couldn't have done it without your collective ability to fall on your swords and allow us to excel.

I sent early versions of the manuscript to various wise souls whose opinions I trust. Their feedback helped me to evaluate and develop the themes and stories that appear in the book. As such, it was essential to the outcome. Particular mentions go to Roger, Harry, Nick, Jamie and Callan, all of whom have been swamped by random messages from me, likely at inopportune times of the day, during this process. Heartfelt thanks. Your support was and remains invaluable.

Kiri, I wrote the first draft of this during lockdown with you. You always believed in what I was trying to do. Without your creativity, love and laughter, it's unlikely this book would have come to fruition.

Jen, my editor, I don't know how you do it! You set the bar high on our previous collaborations. I found this one even more enjoyable. Over the course of our association, I have developed complete trust in your judgement. You improved the story with every insight you offered.

Thanks to my copy editor, Ian, whose input has again been invaluable. I appreciate your effort and the precision you bring to the creative process.

Clare, my agent, the faith you showed in my literary aims was essential. I'm enormously grateful for the massive amount of time and energy you devoted to helping shape the story.

Ian, Ryan, Lauren, Felicity and the rest of the team at Unicorn, it has been a pleasure working with you. Thank you for your belief in the project and your hard work in bringing it all together.

Finally, to my family, you're all amazing! I'm so lucky to have you in my life. Your support in every venture I've embarked upon has been whole-hearted and humbling. Words aren't sufficient.

Glossary

2IC – second-in-command
AOSB – Army Officer Selection Board
CBRN – chemical, biological, radiological and nuclear
CC – commissioning course
COA – course of action
CSM – company sergeant major
DS – Directing Staff
EndEx – end of exercise
FIBUA – Fighting In Built-Up Areas
FF – friendly forces
FOB – Forward Operating Base
HOTO – Handover-Takeover
KFS – knife fork spoon
LOAC – Law of Armed Conflict
O Group – Orders Group
PFA – Personal Fitness Assessment
PO – potential officer
PT – Physical Training
PTI – Physical Training Instructor
PTSD – post-traumatic stress disorder
RAC – Royal Armoured Corps
RMAS – Royal Military Academy Sandhurst
RSB – Regimental Selection Board
SNCO – senior non-commissioned officer
TAB – Tactical Advance to Battle
UOTC – University Officers' Training Corps

Also by Geordie Stewart

A Rolling Stone: Taking the Road Less Travelled, 2020

In Search of Sisu: A Path to Contentment via the Highest Point on Every Continent, 2018